The

GRAND
WEAVER

Books by Ravi Zacharias

Is Your Church Ready?
Motivating Leaders to Live an Apologetic Life
(general editor with Norman Geisler)

Walking from East to West

Who Made God?
And Answers to Over 100 Other Tough Questions of Faith
(general editor with Norman Geisler)

The

GRAND
WEAVER

How God Shapes Us Through
the Events of Our Lives

RAVI
ZACHARIAS

ZONDERVAN.com/
AUTHORTRACKER
follow your favorite authors

The Grand Weaver
Copyright © 2007 by Ravi Zacharias

This title is also available as a Zondervan audio product.
Visit www.zondervan.com/audiopages for more information.

Requests for information should be addressed to:

Zondervan, *Grand Rapids, Michigan* 49530

ISBN-13: 978-0-310-26997-7
ISBN-10: 0-310-26997-0

International Trade Paper Edition

Published in association with the literary agency of Wolgemuth and Associates, Inc.

Interior design by Beth Shagene

Printed in the United States of America

07 08 09 10 11 12 13 • 23 22 21 20 19 18 17 16 15 14 13 12 11 10 9 8 7 6 5 4 3 2 1

To Sarah, Naomi, and Nathan, our beloved children.
Three beautiful tapestries woven by God.
Finish well, Sweethearts.

———

Contents

Introduction

OUT OF THE THOUSANDS OF LETTERS THAT I RECEIVE EACH YEAR, many from skeptics, a recent one stands out. The writer asks simply, "Why has God made it so difficult to believe in him? If I loved somebody and had infinite power, I would use that power to show myself more obviously. Why has God made it so difficult to see his presence and his plan?"

This is a fair and haunting question. Theologians refer to this as "the hiddenness of God." The skeptic uses stronger terms, referring to him as the God who has absconded and left us with no visible sign of his existence.

How do we arrive at any sense in dealing with this struggle? Would anyone deny that they would really like to see some periodic "visitation" from God, some tangible evidence of his existence? And who among us would not like to know his plan?

As much as the question *seems* powerful, however, I contend that the answers we give must remind the questioner that maybe, just maybe, the question itself hasn't been carefully thought through. For example, how often would we want God to reveal himself? Once a day? Every time there is an emergency? Would we like to hear a voice every now and then, saying, "Trust me"? The interesting thing about this demand is that some *have* seen God's presence; some *have* heard his voice—yet it did not make it any easier for them to believe. It turns out that when you are all-powerful, someone will always demand that you demonstrate the fact.

John the Baptist, who introduced the Christ to the world, saw many miracles. Yet when John found himself in prison, he wondered if Jesus really was who he claimed to be. Apparently he thought, "If Jesus is indeed the Christ, then why would he allow me to rot in prison?" Peter had the most dramatic disclosure ever given to the human eye atop the mountain, when he saw the transfiguration of Jesus. He felt so overwhelmed that he did not want to come down again. Yet not long afterwards, when Jesus was arrested and on his way to the cross, Peter denied that he ever knew him.

Cynicism or Climax?

We always like to know how a story ends, don't we? Otherwise we feel cheated. Does a sudden disappointment or unexpected event shatter everything else we believed? Is this disappointment a marker before the turn, or is it the end of the road for us? Carrying the question further—is the end of life the most awesome thing we will ever encounter, or is it a long day's journey into night? If we were to judge by much of what we see and hear, we would honestly find it difficult to keep ourselves from becoming cynical about life. More and more, when something terrible happens, we declare, "That's life!"—as though disappointment and heartache declare the sum total of this existence.

We miss the roses and see only the thorns. We take for granted the warmth of the sun and get depressed by the frequency of the rain or the snow. We ignore the sounds of life in a nursery because we are preoccupied with the sounds of sirens responding to an emergency. We forget the marvel of a marriage that has endured the test of time because we feel discouraged by the heartaches of loved ones whose marriages didn't make it to the end.

In his play "Long Day's Journey into Night," Eugene O'Neill has one of his characters utter a powerful statement toward the end of her life: "None of us can help the things life has done to us. They are done before you realize it and once they are done, they make you do other things, until at last everything comes between you and what you'd like to be, and you've lost your true self forever."[1] Which of us has not flirted with the despair reflected in these sobering lines? Are we really dealt a deck of cards, all predesigned like a magician's pack toward a certain fixed end? Is it just an illusion that we play the game at will?

We must recognize that divine intervention is nowhere near as simple a thing as we might imagine. For it to sustain us and give us staying power—to help us remain firm and see God's hand at every stage of our lives—it must look quite different from what we would usually prescribe for ourselves. It cannot be only a journey of unmistakable blessing and a path of ease. To allow God to be God we must follow him for who he is and what he intends, and not for what we want or what we prefer. That's what this book is about: seeing the designing hand of God and his intervention in our lives in such a way that we know he has a specific purpose for each of us and that he will carry us through until we meet him face-to-face and know ourselves completely.

An Unexpected Face

Some years ago I was speaking in South Africa. I felt fortunate to be there during a major cricket match between South Africa and the West Indies. The manager of the South African team came to one of my speaking engagements, and he was able to get me tickets close to the players' viewing box. I had a marvelous time. As we spoke, he told me of his newfound faith in Jesus Christ.

"It happened in a very strange way," he said. He explained that he had been a confirmed skeptic most of his life and felt quite hostile toward those with any belief in God. Then one Easter Sunday morning, as he sat by his swimming pool, he heard the strains of Easter hymns highlighting Jesus' resurrection coming from a television inside the house. It irritated him. Then at one point, beer in hand, he muttered a whim. "If you really are who you say you are," he demanded, "show yourself to me." That's all he said—really, a bit of a taunt.

No more than a half hour later, as he stared at the pool, he seemed to see the features of Jesus' face as portrayed in famous paintings, sort of rippling on the surface of the water, appearing and then disappearing. At first it startled him. Then he just brushed it off, figuring he had consumed one too many beers.

By the time he woke up early the next morning, he had almost forgotten the experience. But as he walked toward his bathroom, wouldn't you know it, there was that face again, somehow imbedded in the grain of the door. Now it really grabbed his attention. Within the next hour, as he got ready for the day, he saw the same features on three doors in different rooms, suddenly coming together to form the face of Christ— almost like the pieces of a puzzle interlocked in a time-lapsed sequence. He almost became afraid to look at any more doors. It turned out this was all he needed. His life took a turn, and he came to believe that God knew what it was going to take to win him over.

Near the end of our conversation, almost offhandedly, he said something that really piqued my curiosity. "Those images are still as visible on the doors today as they were then," he declared.

"You can see them *today*?" I asked.

"Yes. Would you like to come over this week?"

I jumped at the chance. Talk cricket *and* see a miracle at the same time? To me, that would be as dramatic an evidence of God's intervention as I could have wanted. I said as much to him with a twinkle in my eye and, of course, tongue in cheek. We set the date for my wife and me to have dinner in his home. I could hardly wait.

When the day finally arrived, after the initial pleasantries, I said, "Can I see those images on the doors now?" He delightedly ushered me to the bedroom and took me to the vantage point from where he had made his first sighting. I have to admit that as soon as he positioned me, one look at the grain of the wood and I knew exactly what he was pointing to. "Wow!" I said. "I can see that." I stared and stared, and I could see why a man who wanted such a sign could not miss such a hint. Then we visited the next room. There I had to tilt my head this way and that before I could see any image. The second one seemed a bit blurred and not as convincing. Then the third—a little better than the second, but not as clear as the first. I argued with myself about its empirical power and then left, only half convinced.

We had a wonderful afternoon, chatting as he spoke of his life and his loves. When I left, I asked myself the question, "Was that just the grain of the wood? Could it be that, somehow, if you stared long enough, it looked like a face?" Was it maybe something like seeing a numeric code in every word you read? Or was it really possible that God in his mercy deals with some of us in ways that connect with us individually, so that the means may vary but the ends remain the same—a direct divine encounter bringing conviction to our soul that God is near?

Different for Everyone

Across history, people have come to God through different experiences, but in the end they have seen a designing hand that shaped their lives and their circumstances. And that was enough for them. They trusted God implicitly, without needing a constant "miracle" to keep their faith vibrant.

For me, the last few years have been more an intellectual journey than a material display. The latter has followed, however, and I have seen enough of God's intervention to make me quietly content with his plan and purpose in my life. Sometimes I thought he was silent; now I see he was not. At times I thought he was absent; today I know he was there. He has gently yet unmistakably demonstrated to me, both by argument and by experience, that he is very near and very active.

I believe God intervenes in the lives of *every one of us*. He speaks to us in different ways and at different times so that we may know he is the author of our very personality. And he wants us to know he has a calling for each of us, designed to fulfill each individual's uniqueness. That is why John and Peter and a host of others, in the end, willingly paid the ultimate price, even as they sought God's power and presence in those "dark nights of the soul."[2] In fact, I believe more matters to God in our lives than we normally pause to think about. We may not fully understand his design as it takes shape, but we should not conclude that his design lacks a directing plan.

Breathtaking Beauty

In my mind's eye I see a modest-looking building in the northern city of Varanasi, India. Those who read my autobiographical journey *Walking from East to West* will remember this illustration. In fact, I received so many letters about it that I decided to make it the starting point for this work.

Varanasi is perhaps most famous as the hub of Hinduism, since through it flows the sacred river Ganges. But it also has a deserved reputation for producing the spectacular and breathtaking saris that every bride in northern India wants to wear on her wedding day. Having attended numerous weddings while growing up in Delhi, I well recall admiring these magnificent works of art. The spectacular colors practically explode: reds that seem to be the source from which all other reds emerge; royal blues that look as though they reflect the oceans of the world; brilliant greens that appear to borrow from the finest emeralds and lend their softer side to all the well-manicured lawns of the world; and gold and silver threads that don't just *seem* to be gold and silver because they *are* real gold and silver. All these colors get woven into patterns that one would think came from the perfect mind and the perfect pair of hands. I had always wanted to see how they were made. Who created them, and how did they do it?

I walk into a building and then into a little side room. In typical Indian fashion, the surroundings leave very much to be desired, but the final product is nothing short of a work of art. Essentially, a father and son team makes each sari. The father sits on a raised platform with huge spools of brilliantly colored threads within his reach. The son sits on the floor in the lotus position (with apparent ease and comfort I can only envy—the first challenge would be to get into that position and the second to stand up afterwards). The team wears basic and simple clothing. Their fingers move nimbly, their hands never touching any softening lotion. They hunch over their work, and their eyes focus on the pattern emerging with each move of the shuttle.

Before my eyes, though it did not appear so at first, a grand design appears. The father gathers some threads in his hand, then nods, and the son moves the shuttle from one side to the other. A few more threads, another nod, and again the son responds by moving the shuttle. The process seems almost Sisyphus-like in its repetition, the silence broken only occasionally with a comment or by some visitor who interrupts to ask a question about the end design. The father smiles and tries in broken English to explain the picture he has in his mind, but compared to the magnificence of the final product, it is a mere lisp. I know that if I were to come back a few weeks later—in some instances a few months later—I would see the spools of thread almost empty and a six-yard-long sari, breathtaking in all of its splendor.

Throughout the process, the son has had a much easier task. Most likely he has often felt bored. Perhaps his back has ached or his legs have gone to sleep. Perhaps he has wished for some other calling in life—something he might find more stimulating or fulfilling. He has but one task, namely, to move the shuttle as directed by the father's nod, hoping to learn to think like the father so that he can carry on the business at the appropriate time.

Yet the whole time, the design has remained in the mind of the father as he held the threads. In a few days, this sari will make its way to a shop in Delhi or Bombay or Calcutta. A lovely young lady with her mother will note the saris on display. This one will catch her eye and she will exclaim, "*Bohut badiya* [how grand]! *Khupsurat* [what a beautiful face]!" A sari with a beautiful face, because a grand weaver has purposefully designed it. Before long, it will be draped around her, beautifying the lovely bride.

Now if an ordinary weaver can take a collection of colored threads and create a garment to beautify the face, is it not possible that the Grand Weaver has a design in mind for *you*, a design that will adorn you as he uses your life to fashion you for his purpose, using all the threads within his reach?

Still in Tune

One little stanza of an Isaac Watts' hymn illustrates God's majesty, expressed in the unique way he has made each one of us:

Our life contains a thousand springs,
and dies if one be gone;
strange that a harp of a thousand strings
should keep in tune so long![3]

Once you begin to see God's hand in your life, you will know that his workmanship within you and through you was tailor-made, just for you. His design for your life pulls together every thread of your existence into a magnificent work of art. Every thread matters and has a specific purpose.

I pray that as you read these pages, you will see those threads come together and know that God is indeed the Grand Weaver of your life.

RAVI K. ZACHARIAS

CHAPTER 1

Your DNA Matters

MY FATHER-IN-LAW PASSED AWAY A MERE THREE MONTHS BEFORE I began to pen these words. His downward slide had begun a few weeks before, when what started as an ordinary day ended with life's sunset in sight.

He felt bothered by an odd feeling in his lower back and chalked it up to a muscle strain. But as the pain intensified, he scheduled a visit to see his doctor, just to make sure there wasn't any skeletal damage. As the doctor did a casual examination, poking around and feeling the inflammation, he didn't like what he felt. He directed my father-in-law to the hospital across the street for some tests.

Several days later the reason for the pain became clear: a fast-growing tumor was impinging on the kidney. The prognosis was grim.

Before this moment he had no intimation of anything so fearsome. And yet, less than five months later we buried him — and the heavens opened up and wept with us.

A severe time of testing descended on the whole family right after this diagnosis was made. Emotions swung from slender glimmers of hope when it looked as though he just might make it, to a dark foreboding that the end was near. We had all taken the opportunity to get some time alone with him. My children wrote long personal letters to express their deep love and great admiration for him.

As the end drew near, the days grew heavy emotionally. Three of his four daughters and his wife cared for him every moment of the last week of his life. When his daughters tried to comfort him by assuring him that they would be there to take care of him, with quivering lip he said, "You don't know what you are saying. Taking care of a dying person can be very unpleasant."

My father-in-law had seen his mother care for his grand-mother before she died, you see, and he knew what might be coming. To make things even more difficult, he was probably the most gentlemanly of all the gentlemen I ever knew. He had a perfect sense of propriety in every situation—ever the right demeanor, ever the right word. Just a year before, he had helped bury his only brother. After the graveside service, he quietly spoke with a few people. Suddenly he became aware that the cemetery staff had begun to lower the casket containing his brother's remains into the ground. He gently ended the conver-sation and stood at attention until earth had completely filled in the grave. He was a man of immense dignity—and this was the man who now himself lay dying, tormented by the added fear of the indignities he suspected might be awaiting him.

His body had become small and thin, his mind no longer able to think rationally. He could not communicate, and his very blue eyes remained either closed or unfocused. He could not even keep his clothes on. My wife said that one of the hard-est things about watching him die was seeing this man of such vast dignity reduced to … *this*. Finally, they watched him take his last tortured breath, and he was gone.

But something incredible happened in the last few moments of his life. Until this day, it gives me pause, as it did those who were with him. It helped put everything in perspective. But this I shall save for later.

If, however, the only thing that had taken place is what I have described already, then how could we escape the difficult questions? Are we all moving toward an inglorious end? What is the meaning of life, if it ends with such helplessness and loss of dignity?

An Odd Mix of Order and Surprise

I begin with this story of my father-in-law's passing because every aspect of his personality came into focus during those last days. This was one man, up against his greatest fears. As his doctor said, "He was a man of faith; yet faith didn't come easily to him."

At the same time that he faced his greatest fears, some of his greatest hopes came to fulfillment. He had planned, organized, and labeled practically everything in his life. One look at his clothes, his files, and his daily life, and you would envy a man so meticulous in every detail. Yet, in the end, the planning was not of his doing.

In this odd mix of order and surprise, enchantment and hurt, we long for some sense. Can we detect some intentionally woven pattern here? Is the human story "a tale told by an idiot, full of sound and fury, signifying nothing," as Shakespeare said?[1] Or is there a grand design, not just for life but for each individual life—yours and mine? Could the words of Canadian World War II pilot John Gillespie Magee be more appropriate?

> *Oh, I have slipped the surly bonds of earth*
> *And danced the skies on laughter-silvered wings ...*
> *Put out my hand and touched the face of God.*[2]

The Bible offers a beautiful passage from the heart of one who knew much, suffered much, endured much, and wrote much:

"No eye has seen,
*   no ear has heard,*
no mind has conceived
*   what God has prepared for those who love him."*

1 CORINTHIANS 2:9

If this is true, then such awe-inspiring consolation reaches beyond the future to carry profound implications for the present. If God has prepared something for me that will literally take my breath away, then even though he plans to give me a new kind of body and mind, he must have a specific purpose for my body and mind here as well.

The question is, How can you see the divine intersection of all that shapes and marks your existence, whether it be the heart-wrenching tragedies that wound you or the ecstasy of a great delight that brings laughter to your soul? How can you meet God in all your appointments and your disappointments? How can you recognize that he has a purpose, even when all around seems senseless, if not hopeless? Will there be a last gasp that whispers in one word a conclusion that redefines everything? If so, is it possible to borrow from that word to enrich the now? Can we really see, even a little, the patterned convergence of everything into some grand design?

To See or Not to See?

Right here we run into our first stray thread. Many of us would not have chosen for ourselves the body or face or features that we have. In fact, we might often wish to be unburdened with the physicality of our being. With the importance given today to having a beautiful or "perfect" body, some might wonder why they ended up with theirs. Why this body and not another? "If only I could shake it off," we muse. In fact, why have a body at all, since it can be so uncomfortable to bear?

Even as a child, when you read the fairy tale of "Jack the Giant Killer," you knew right from the start that Jack could do what he did only because he had that marvelous coat. Each time he draped it over himself, his body became invisible, allowing him to defeat the giant and so proving the adage that you cannot hit what you cannot see. How could Jack have vanished from that bone-littered dungeon? How could he have stolen away with the beautiful princess? How could all those ferocious monsters that sought his scalp fail in their murderous attempts? It was that enchanted coat! All Jack had to do was to throw it over his shoulders, and he became invisible — transcending and neutralizing the body at the same time.[3]

Who of us at some time has not wanted a coat like that? And fairy tale writers aren't the only ones who imagine a tool with such powers. Did not Plato in *The Republic* introduce us to Gyges, who discovered a wonderful ring? Whenever he slipped it on and pointed it in a certain direction, his body ceased to hinder him. Even Plato, with his famous metaphor of shadows, found time in his thoughts to imagine life without a body.[4] Ah! what marvels we could do if we could get a ring like that. It's the stuff movies are made of.

In more recent times, H. G. Wells wrote of the "Invisible Man." Here it was not a coat or a ring but a chemical concoction that one could drink to become invisible. Listen to his description:

> I shall never forget that dawn, and the strange horror of seeing that my hands had become as clouded glass, and watching them grow clearer and thinner as the days went by, until at last I could see the sickly disorder of my room through them, though I closed my transparent eyelids. My limbs became glassy, the bones and arteries faded, vanished, and the little white nerves went last. I gritted my teeth and stayed there to the end. At last only the dead tips of the fingernails

remained, pallid and white, and the brown stain of some acid upon my fingers.[5]

From science fiction to philosophy to fairy tales, we dream of being able to make ourselves invisible at will, sometimes for good reasons but sometimes for all of the wrong ones. And that is an important clue.

The enchanted coat and the ring of Gyges and the chemical concoction present some terrible possibilities, don't they? What if a criminal had a coat like that? What if a mass murderer had a concoction like that? The power of invisibility would mean the ultimate destruction of humanity, for criminals would certainly abuse and misuse it and so wreak catastrophic havoc with it.

We identify and recognize individuals via the body. With all of our misgivings, the body is both individual and identifiable. But it is more than that.

A Name or a Number

Pause here with me and consider this: the body—the face, the features, the coloring—contains marks that identify us as individuals. These marks arise from our DNA and make us recognizable to the naked eye. But they provide more than a point of recognition for the sake of others; they are God's imprint on each of us. These few features have seemingly infinite possibilities when rearranged in different shapes and sizes. And how often each of us vents and complains to God, either implicitly or explicitly, wanting a better personal design: "If only I had a stronger back to do what I need to do!" "If only I had a more powerful voice that would convey authority!"

Even those we regard as heroes of the faith have not escaped such thoughts. In the Old Testament, God called Moses to lead the Israelites out of Egypt, but Moses kept coming up with all kinds of excuses for why he was a poor choice. To Moses' observation that he was "slow of speech and tongue," God said, "Who gave man his mouth?" in effect asking, "Who made *your* mouth, Moses?" (see Exodus 4:10–11). Granted, God designed the question to remind Moses that since God had made his mouth, God could use it as he saw fit; but the point is well taken. We are fearfully and wonderfully made. Every time we make something artificial to duplicate what we have or had naturally, we once more recognize the intricate nature of the design, even with its weaknesses.

My daughter Naomi works with the destitute of the world and others trapped in and sold into the sex-trafficking industry. She wears a black pearl pendant around her neck, a gift from a friend. There's a story behind that gift. When the friend saw it in a store, she commented that the pearls had some odd markings. "Yes," said the clerk, "some see them as flawed; others see them as special." That was all Naomi's friend needed to hear. She bought it for Naomi to remind her that the hurting individuals she serves are not flawed but unique and special.

The recent movie *The March of the Penguins* features an awe-inspiring scene in which the males return with food after having been gone for weeks. As the biting winds of winter begin to take their toll and time starts to run out, the males, thousands of them, return, almost as if in a regiment commanded by a general. They waddle back to their "home" amid the thousands of females there, each calling for her mate, and in the midst of that cacophony of sound, each male begins the search for his own partner and offspring—his unique ones.

This is not just nature. This is the Grand Weaver designing the thoughts and the instinct to bring order out of chaos—to bring order out of the chaos we have created for ourselves in our attempts to shake off our bodies by the use of enchanted coats or rings or chemicals. When these birds from the movie reunite, they share a tender moment, revealing that all this individuality and identifiability had a purpose for each one. The penguins may not be able to articulate all that it means to them, but in analogous situations—as well as in dissimilar circumstances—humans can and do.

In Chiang Mai, Thailand, you will find a house called "Ban Sanook." It literally means "Fun House." As you enter, you see a group of people of varying ages involved in weaving. Here, for example, is twenty-five-year-old Bodintr Bain. His demeanor, his bouncing walk, and his contagious smile make you want to pull a chair over and watch him at work. His friends call him Tu. Tu looks up, smiles and says, "I'm weaving a giant wave. I want to weave colorful patterns of waves and make the cloth as big as the wide ocean, so that I'll have enough space to play and swim in my dreams." Laughter fills his voice. He uses "Saori," the Japanese technique of weaving, to do his work. Twelve of his friends surround him, each doing the same thing, yet each with a different design in mind. They dream up their designs and fulfill their yearnings in this fun-filled home.

But what makes it so special? Of the thirteen here, three have physical disabilities, six have Down syndrome (including Tu), one is autistic, and the other three have learning or developmental disabilities. As you talk to Tu, you notice a bright-eyed woman standing nearby, watching his moves and listening to his descriptions of his work. Then she gently interjects her own words: "This is my son. He has now sold sixty of his creations. When he receives the payment for each one, he hands it to me and says, 'This is yours because without you I never would have made it.'"

Even in his debilitation, he knows that neither the work of art nor his life itself would have occurred but for the mother who conceived him, carried him, and loved him, Down syndrome and all. Now as he "creates," he recognizes and acknowledges that ultimately she is the one who has made his creations possible, and so he brings his earnings and sets them at her feet.

What a picture this is, I thought, of the climactic moment of our earthly life when we bow before God. I have a feeling we will be saying the same thing that Tu says to his mother.

So I ask again—if a man who experiences such limited access to his own mental capacities can do such incredible work, how much more grand is the work of our Heavenly Father as he pulls together all the varied strands of life to reveal his grand design? Sometimes he uses soft and delicate colors; at other times he chooses dramatic and vibrant ones.

In the book *Finding Your Way*, Gary LaFerla tells an amazing story, gleaned from the records of the United States Naval Institute following the Second World War. The USS *Astoria* engaged the Japanese during the battle for Savo Island before any other ships from the U.S. naval fleet arrived. During the crucial night of the battle, August 8, the *Astoria* scored several direct hits on a Japanese vessel but was itself badly damaged and sank the next day. Here's how LaFerla tells the rest of the story:

> About 0200 hours a young Midwesterner, Signalman 3rd Class Elgin Staples, was swept overboard by the blast when the *Astoria's* number one eight-inch gun turret exploded. Wounded in both legs by shrapnel and semi-shock, he was kept afloat by a narrow lifebelt that he managed to activate with a simple trigger mechanism.
>
> At around 0600 hours, Staples was rescued by a passing destroyer and returned to the *Astoria*, whose captain was attempting to save the cruiser by beaching her. The effort failed, and Staples, still wearing the same lifebelt, found himself back in the water. It was lunchtime. Picked up again, this time by the USS *President Jackson* (AP–37), he was one of 500 survivors of the battle who were evacuated to Noumea. On board the transport, Staples hugging that lifebelt with gratitude, looked at that small piece of

equipment for the first time. He scrutinized every stitch of the lifebelt that had served him so well. It had been manufactured by Firestone Tire and Rubber Company of Akron, Ohio, and bore a registration number.

Given home leave, Staples told his story and asked his mother, who worked for Firestone, about the purpose of the number on the belt. She replied that the company insisted on personal responsibility for the war effort, and that the number was unique and assigned to only one inspector. Staples remembered everything about the lifebelt, and quoted the number. There was a moment of stunned silence in the room and then his mother spoke: "That was my personal code that I affixed to every item I was responsible for approving."[6]

I can only imagine the emotions within the hearts of mother and son as they pondered the convergence of responsibility and its impact on life. The threads had come together in an inescapable way. The one who gave him birth and whose DNA he bore gave him rescue in the swirling waters that threatened to take his life. If an earthly parent playing the role of procreation can provide a means of rescue without knowing when and for whom that belt would come into play, how much more can the God of all creation accomplish? By his sovereign will, we have come into being with an expressed and designed purpose.

To be able to accept the wonder and the marvel of one's own personality, however flawed or "accidental," and place it in and trust it to the hands of the One who made it, is one of the greatest achievements in life. His "registration number" is on you. Your DNA matters because the essence of who you are matters and whose you are by design matters. Every little feature and "accident" of your personality matter. Consider it God's sovereign imprint on you.

The often-heard comment "a face only a mother could love" reflects more fact than cynicism. God loves you as one who loves his own offspring. Your face is unique because your DNA is unique. When you finally meet the One who made you and examine the lifelines he has sent you along the way, you will at last understand how every detail made sense in the swirling reality of life's blessings and threats. They will speak of God's transcending love for you.

The Book of Life in Pictures

Some time ago I had the privilege to speak at a conference at Johns Hopkins University on the theme "What Does It Mean to Be Human?" Before my address, Francis Collins, the director of the Human Genome Project and the co-mapper of human DNA, presented his talk. He spoke of the intelligibility and marvel of the book of life, filled with more than three billion bits of information. In a strange way, he became both the subject and the object of his study, both the designer and the design of his research. Extraordinary thoughts swarmed within me as I listened, virtually tuning in and out of the talk in order to reflect on the wonder of it all.

In his last slide, he showed two pictures side by side. On the left appeared a magnificent photo of the stained-glass rose window from Yorkminster Cathedral in Yorkshire, England, its symmetry radiating from the center, its colors and geometric patterns spectacular—clearly a work of art purposefully designed by a gifted artist. Its sheer beauty stirred the mind. On the right side of the screen appeared a slide showing a cross section of a strand of human DNA. The picture did more than take away one's breath; it was awesome in the profoundest sense of the term—not just beautiful, but overwhelming. And it almost mirrored the pattern of the rose window in Yorkminster. The intricacy of the DNA's design, which pointed to the

Transcendent One, astonished those who are themselves the design and who have been created semitranscendent by design. We see ourselves only partially, but through our Creator's eyes, we see our transcendence. In looking at our own DNA, the subject and the object came together.

The audience gasped at the sight, for it saw itself. The design, the color, the splendor of the design left everyone speechless, even though it is this very design that makes us capable of speech. Because of this design we can think in profound ways, but we felt paralyzed by the thought and could go no further. Because of that design we remained trapped in time but were momentarily lifted to the eternal. Because of that design we were capable of love and suddenly could see the loveliness of who we are.

We can map out the human genome and in it see the evidence of a great Cartographer. We can plan and now see a great Planner. We can sing and now see poetry in matter. We speculate and see the intricacies of purpose. We live, seeing the blueprint of life. And we die, but we can look through the keyhole of life.

At Johns Hopkins that day we saw the handiwork of the One who made us for himself—and when we grasp its splendor, we find the greatest joy of all to be the truth that every thread matters and contributes to the adornment of the bride of the One who became flesh for us and dwelt among us.

The day that each person willingly accepts himself or herself for who he or she is and acknowledges the uniqueness of God's framing process marks the beginning of a journey to seeing the handiwork of God in each life. Trying to mirror someone else's accomplishments is one thing. Trying to be someone else in distinctive capacity is unhealthy and breeds insatiable hungers. Not everyone is a Bach or an Einstein. But there is splendor in the ordinary. The mother who made the lifebelt is worthy of recognition equal to Bach. Her labor of love is as unique as discovering $E = MC^2$, Einstein's famous formula. This is why seeing one's self through God's grand design is essential to completing the picture for all of creation. We must have a healthy respect for our individuality but also keep a wise distance from it. We have it now, but it is not what we shall be. C. S. Lewis, in his brilliant way, reminds us of this:

> Most of man's psychological make-up is probably due to his body: when his body dies all that will fall off him, and the real central man, the thing that chose, that made the best or worst of this material, will stand naked. All sorts of nice things which we thought our own, but which were really due to a good digestion, will fall off some of us; all sorts of nasty things which were due to complexities or bad health will fall off others. We shall then for the first time, see every one as he really was. There will be surprises.[7]

At the beginning of this chapter, I mentioned that my father-in-law did something utterly unforgettable in the final days of his life. As strength was leaving his body and he could no longer communicate with loved ones, he suddenly opened his eyes and said twice, quietly and clearly, "Amazing! It's just amazing!" A few hours later, he again stirred, reached out his thin arms to his wife of sixty-two years, and said, "I love you!" Then he let his head drop back on his pillow. Those were his last words. Within twenty-four hours he was gone. That was the end.

Or was it the beginning? When you know the Grand Weaver, it is neither. It was a punctuation mark in the design that he was about to see and enjoy forever.

Accepting and celebrating the thread of your own personality is the first grasp of the Grand Weaver's design in your life. You are not a number. He knows you by name. Every stage of the process may not look picturesque, but every detail will come into focus and possess its share of beauty.

CHAPTER 2

Your Disappointments Matter

SOMETIMES LIFE SUDDENLY JOLTS US LIKE AN ENGINE STOPPING IN midair. Some years ago, my assistant approached me after I had finished a task in our recording studio and announced, "Margie wants to see you right away." By the tone of her statement, I knew that something serious had happened.

I picked up my pace as I walked toward my wife's office down the hall. Immediately I noticed the closed door—the next clue that something had gone wrong. Her door is *always* open. I opened the door and saw tears streaming down her face. I walked over to her side, put my arm around her, and asked, "What's the matter?"

"Robert Fraley just died in a plane crash!"

That was all she needed to say. My heart sank as I heard her words. Robert Fraley was a very dear friend. Many who do not know his name may still recall the story because it made international news.

On October 25, 1999, shortly after 9 a.m., a Lear jet took off from Orlando, Florida, on a business trip, carrying two pilots and four passengers. The best-known passenger on the flight was golfer Payne Stewart, the U.S. Open winner that year. Robert Fraley served as Stewart's agent, as he did for many other prominent sports figures. Shortly after takeoff, the plane veered off course, and air traffic controllers lost voice contact with the pilot. Military aircraft promptly took to the air and approached the jet, reporting that its windows had iced over. Repeated attempts to make contact failed, and ground experts deduced that the aircraft's pressurization mechanism had malfunctioned. The Air Force fighters trailed the stricken plane for four hours, even when it soared as high as forty-five thousand feet. Halfway across the United States, the pilotless plane ran out of fuel, and the aircraft, with all six on board already dead, nose-dived at a ninety-degree angle into a field in Minot, South Dakota. Tortured loved ones watched as this surreal event unfolded before their eyes.

Many people counted Robert Fraley a gracious and generous friend, a man of rare gentlemanly qualities. All who knew him esteemed him. His funeral testified to a life magnificently lived. Those who knew him well felt shattered by this dramatic loss of a young life. His wife, Dixie, bore the scars of his death with anguished dignity, as did the other widows.

One cannot but raise the question, as harsh as it sounds, Why do so many destructive people live to a ripe old age, while so many who dedicate themselves to serving others and God seem to get snuffed out so soon? Does anyone who observes life philosophically not at some stage ask this question? This is not merely the "why" of tragedy but the "why" of unequal justice. We can almost accept a punitive explanation if the apparent retribution came to someone whose life merited it. But what about those who walk the straight and narrow, whose lives consistently bless others? Why does the harshness of tragedy strike *them*?

The questions reveal the simplistic nature of our analyses and conclusions—as if we know all there is to know. We immediately start asking questions about retribution and judgment, as if that could really explain it. Somebody had to have sinned, we think, for a man to be born blind (see John 9:2). Something had to be wrong in a person's life for a marriage to have broken up. Why else would bad things happen? So goes our reasoning. The problem of pain has remained the single greatest question, not only for the skeptic who uses it as an excuse to doubt God's existence, but also for the believer who questions God's purpose.

Pain, Despair, and Golden Windows

Some time ago, during a visit to see a relative in India, we began talking about an extraordinary tragedy in our family. My cousin had died in his hotel room while in his early forties due to an overreaction to a medication. My aunt explained how it all happened as I listened. A friend who had attended my cousin's funeral sat quietly but with evident grief. Finally my aunt said, "This lady has a memory from that funeral that none of us will ever forget." In the midst of the funeral, this friend had been pondering the plight of the mother who had just lost her son. "What a terrible thing it must be to cope with this," she had thought. Unknown to her, at that very hour, her own son perished in a fatal car accident. She received news of his death later that evening. So she suffered a double devastation—first, to witness and ponder a friend's terrible grief, and then to experience a similar horror herself.

Talk about pain, and you never lack for listeners. Ruth Graham, the daughter of Billy and Ruth Bell Graham, has written a book rightly titled *In Every Pew Sits a Broken Heart*. Three-quarters of the way through the book, my heart sank, and I thought, "How can one person live with so much pain?" Every month, hurting inquirers inundate her website, asking for help.

Over the years, I have discovered that pain, like despair, comes not in one package or one expression but in various measures. While pain is the universal leveler, it works differently in everyone's life. It shapes us uniquely, sparing no one in the process. Even as we writhe under its blows, we assume that no one else can possibly have gone through what we have endured.

Do you remember the old story of the house with the golden windows? It tells of a little boy who would look across the sprawling meadows outside his house every morning and see in the distance a house with golden windows. He would stare and revel in the radiant beams streaming his way from far away. He asked his father one day if they could visit the house with the golden windows. The father obliged, and they started to walk. They walked and walked until they approached the house. The young lad stood perplexed. He saw no windows of gold. But a little girl inside saw them staring at her home and came out to ask if they were looking for something. "Yes," replied the boy, "I wanted to see the house with the golden windows that I see every morning."

"Oh, you've come to the wrong place," she quickly said. "If you wait here a little while until sunset, I will show you the house with the golden windows that I see every evening." She then pointed to a house in the distance — the home of the little boy.[1]

How true this little story is. We go through life looking out of the windows of our own experience, dreaming of a golden window in the distance. But when we look through the windows of the soul, we realize that those distant golden windows do not exist. We see gold only because of the way the light catches our earthly dwellings at different times of our experience, at different times in our lives.

Growing up in India, I recall looking at magazines from America or Canada or England and thinking that life must be so beautiful there — the touched-up pictures of Western icons, the latest model cars, the power to earn a comfortable living, the latest gadgets. Then I moved to the West and made Canada and later the United States my home. I enjoyed the gadgets, drove the cars, ate at fine hotels. But something had changed within me. Yes, I had some hints of catching the light reflected off the comforts I experienced. But the golden windows still remained over the hill. I saw some men and women luxuriating in a lifestyle that made mine look impoverished.

Eventually I began to get invitations to speak to some of those groups. They sent planes to pick me up, aircraft that had their own private landing strips. The meetings would begin and the questions would come. Then someone would ask if they could talk privately—and the mask would come off. The lifestyles of the rich and famous are half-truths. Yes, they live in grander houses, but inside they breathe the same sorrows and have the same longings.

On one occasion, I spoke to a group of professional athletes, fine specimens of humanity. As I walked into the room, I had the awful feeling that I alone had failed the physical. I spoke for thirty minutes, just before a big game. When I finished, one by one they came and thanked me. But one man, who made more money in one game than I did in a year, embraced me, weeping at all he'd lost in the pursuit of prowess and fame.

Since those early days I have sat inside many houses with golden windows. Do you know what I have discovered? Despite the gold, the residents suffer from the same decay of the body, the same longings of the heart, and the same agonies of the soul as everyone else.

Sometimes our hurts or disappointments do only slight damage, while sometimes they inflict deep and devastating wounds. If disappointment were a thief, it would be no respecter of persons. In fact, the more a person had, the more there would be to plunder. So how could there be a Grand Weaver behind the scenes, weaving a pattern such as this?

Is it possible to see a pattern developing and then respond to the nod or the stops? At first, of course, we question the Sovereign One in whose hands our destinies lie: "Who sinned, this man or his parents?" Jesus' own disciples asked this question regarding a man blind from birth. In an amazing way, Jesus turned the question back to them. Those who had physical sight but no vision of the soul were actually the blind ones, Jesus said, for at least the physically blind person knew his disability, whereas the spiritually blind person had no inkling of his greater disability. Then Jesus added that this man's blindness had nothing to do with his own sin or with his parents' sin, but that God intended to use it to display his own work (see John 9).

What is this "work of God"? Such a question makes it easy to get trapped into philosophical discussions that, in the end, leave one with only the abstract. In this book, I do not intend to wander along this path; I have addressed the theoretical side of the question in previous books and articles. Here I simply want to see the appointments God makes with each of us individually in the disappointments of our lives—both the threads that he brings in and the ones that he leaves out, the snagged stitches and the "flaws" that show up at all the "wrong times." This is where we will find the distinctive shape and imprint of the Master Weaver.

Taking a Step

Every journey requires deliberate steps. I believe we need to take three distinct steps in this journey before the pattern becomes visible and we begin to see the work of God. The first involves the *heart*.

God is the shaper of your heart. By the "heart" I do not mean the physical organ, but that which you feel, physically. Have you ever physically felt something you heard or saw close at hand? I do not refer merely to something psychosomatic or to something with a trickle-down impact that leads to an actual disease. I'm talking about an instant transference from thought to body.

A very successful businessman friend of mine who had invested in all kinds of enterprises at one point saw his fortunes start to turn downward. His partner in one major venture, seeing him in distress and in need of some liquidity, offered to buy him out and get him some much-needed cash. My friend was grateful, and over the course of many months the two of them hammered out all the details of the terms. Finally, after completing all the negotiating and compromising that takes place over a major sale, the day came to close the deal. My friend arrived at his partner's office, where they sat down together and had a cup of coffee. But when my friend laid out all the signed papers, his partner said, "I'm sorry to break this news to you, but a few days ago I decided I could not follow through on this. The deal is off."

One look into his eyes told my friend that the man meant what he had said. He also knew he had reached the end of the line. Instantly and with equal shock, he convulsed and slumped over his chair, having suffered a major stroke. His partner stared in horror as the ambulance came and carried the man away on a stretcher. Thankfully, his life was spared, and over time he achieved a partial recovery.

Years later, my friend still struggled even to recount the story to me. He stuttered and stammered and even feigned chuckles along the way. But the pain had scarred him for life. Thankfully, an amazing thing happened in the midst of it. Both his partner, who had become hardened over time through his own wheeling and dealing, and my friend, who had been a tough, emotionless individual, came face-to-face with feeling and with reality.

God does not display his work in abstract terms. He prefers the concrete, and this means that at the end of your life one of three things will happen to your heart: it will grow hard, it will be broken, or it will be tender. Nobody escapes. Your heart will become coarse and desensitized, be crushed under the weight of disappointment, or be made tender by that which makes the heart of God tender as well. God's heart is a caring heart. As the writer of the letter to the Hebrews reminds us, our infirmities deeply touch God (see Hebrews 2:14–18; 4:14–5:3).

This, I believe, explains why the Bible refers to King David as a man after God's own heart (see 1 Samuel 13:14; Acts 13:22). It uses this description not because he led a perfect life (the Scriptures make it very evident that he did not) but because God could reach him in the midst of his failures and his tragedies. This "sweet singer of Israel" had a heart tender enough, when confronted by the prophet, to see that he and not another had committed the sins of adultery and murder (see 2 Samuel 12:13).

God the Grand Weaver seeks those with tender hearts so that he can put his imprint on them. Your hurts and your disappointments are part of that design, to shape your heart and the way you feel about reality. The hurts you live through will always shape you. There is no other way.

One fascinating verse tells us that the author of our salvation himself has been made "perfect through suffering" (Hebrews 2:10). I have often pondered this text. How is One who is already perfect, perfected? Why did the Provision for our malady have to be made less in order to finish the task? I have concluded that while some perfections can never change through all eternity, other perfections are time laden, not only for the one demonstrating it, but, more important, for the completion of the one witnessing it.

For example, the Bible calls Job a perfect man ("blameless and upright," Job 1:1). How could he earn such a description if he had not yet been subjected to the tests necessary for perfection? In his wisdom, God allowed the test not only to shape Job but also to give to us who come after him an example of how an upright person works his way through pain and hurt. Job already had an upright character, but through his struggles we observe how an upright person behaves in the midst of tragedy. That's how the work of God gets displayed.

Perfection, then, is not a change in the essential character but the completion of a course. This is precisely what Jesus must have meant when he admonished both his disciples and us to "be perfect," as our Heavenly Father is perfect (Matthew 5:48). We can never be who God is, but we can complete the task he assigns us to do. Jesus demonstrated that the best way to reach God's desired end is always to obey the will of the Father, even when he seems distant.

Remember how Habakkuk pleaded with God to explain how God could use a terrible people like the Babylonians as the judgment rod against God's own people? Habakkuk literally screamed out the words, "Violence! Injustice! Evil! How can you do this?" (see Habakkuk 1:2–4). But he waited patiently for the Lord to answer until God finally repositioned his view.

Only if you are willing to pray sincerely for God's will to be done and are willing to live the life apportioned to you will you see the breathtaking view of God that he wants you to have, through the windows he has placed in your life. You cannot always live on the mountaintop, but when you walk through the valley, the memory of the view from the mountain will sustain you and give you the strength to carry you through.

Calvin Miller describes the way God answers such pleas for help in tough times:

> The sermon and the Spirit always work in combination to produce liberation. Sometimes the Spirit and sermon do supply direct answers to human need, but most often they answer indirectly. Most problems are not solved by listening to sermons. The sermon, no matter how sincere, cannot solve these unsolvable problems. So if the sermon is not a

problem solver, where shall we go for solutions? Together with the Spirit, the sermon exists to point out that having answers is not essential to living. What is essential is the sense of God's presence during dark seasons of questioning.... Our need for specific answers is dissolved in the greater issue of the lordship of Christ over all questions — those that have answers and those that don't.[2]

A heart in close communion with God helps carry you through the pain, beyond the power of mere words.

Beginning to Walk

The second step involves the *mind*. You get past the stepping out and enter the race, where you watch the signposts carefully.

Neuroscience, the discipline and the enchantment of the hour, prompts us to think only of the brain and pay little attention to the mind. Writers in various fields of science insist that *this* is the hill to climb and the terrain to map. If we can but explain everything that we think and feel through electrochemical signals that send us into thought and conclusion, then we will have the explanation for every behavior. Planting a thought, tantalizing the imagination, engendering an impulse, forming a habit, and shaping the memory — that's the general sequence we seem to follow. And so we see this enchanted loom called the brain now being studied as the originator and storehouse of all behavior.

As much as the subject entices me, I shall resist digression. I simply want to make a reference by analogy. What the brain is to the body, the mind is to the soul. The mind moves beyond fragments of information and puts content together within a context of precommitted factual and moral reason. The mind is not a vacuum. It processes every new bit of information and organizes it into a pattern. When that pattern gets fragmented, we say a person is "losing his mind."

Faith is a thing of the mind. If you do not believe that God is in control and has formed you for a purpose, then you will flounder on the high seas of purposelessness, drowning in the currents and drifting further into nothingness. I pondered, one day, as I read the story of Noah (see Genesis 6:9–22). Read it again. The Bible supplies every detail of the ark: how high, how wide, what kind of wood—the comprehensive blueprint. Yet two details are conspicuously absent: no sail and no rudder. Imagine preparing to float on water for that many days with nothing to control the direction of the ship!

Some time ago, I read a comical quip about a very nervous elderly woman taking her first airplane flight. As the aircraft bounced its way through moderate turbulence, the lady felt certain she was about to die. When the aircraft finally reached calmer air, the pilot stepped out of the cockpit and knelt beside her. "Madam," he asked her, "do you see that light on the end of the right wingtip?"

"Yes," she stammered.

"Now look out of the other window at the left wingtip. Do you see the light on the left wingtip?"

"Yes," again came the nervous answer.

"You know what, Ma'am," the pilot continued, "so long as we stay between those two lights, you have no reason to worry."

Such self-referencing guides are supposed to make us feel better. We think that if only we were in control, everything would be fine. I have a friend who is terrified of flying because, he says, he cannot handle anything that he cannot control. I did not want to offend him by saying, "Welcome to life." God has made it imperative in the design of life that we become willing to trust beyond ourselves. Walking by faith means to follow Someone else who knows more than we do, Someone who is also good.

Essayist F. W. Boreham reminds us that, far from being a childish and uniformed thing, faith is actually the mainspring of the universe, the sheet anchor of civilization. It lies at the heart of all negotiations and worldwide relations. All sound finance builds on it. When people clutch their money, thinking they have concrete reality, they are, in fact, clutching to faith. Money, in that sense, has no value without trust. It is all worthless paper without the promises and pledges of other people and systems. The entire financial structure depends on credit, trust, confidence, belief, and faith. So if America boasts that she is one of the richest countries in the world, she is really boasting about faith. The American academic commits the ultimate self-contradiction by denying that he or she can live by faith—faith and trust are that foundational. That's where the mind takes over and places trust in context. When the mind refuses to trust, even given a context, life becomes pitiable.

The nineteenth-century poet Frances Browne tells of a band of pilgrims sitting by the ocean, sharing with each other their lives and their losses. One speaks of a child who died very young. One tells of a lost fortune. Another mourns a buried wife:

> *But when their tales were done,*
> *There spake among them one,*
> *A stranger seeming from all sorrow free:*
> *"Sad losses have ye met,*
> *But mine is heavier yet,*
> *For a believing heart hath gone from me."*
>
> *"Alas!" these pilgrims said,*
> *"For the living and the dead,*
> *For fortune's cruelty, for love's sure cross,*
> *For the wrecks of land and sea!*
> *But however it came to thee,*
> *Thine, stranger, is life's last and heaviest loss!*
> *For the believing heart has gone from thee."*[3]

The loss of faith is a dreadful thing because it takes away hope and even threatens love. When Noah faced the prospect of a catastrophic flood, he never imagined a boat without a rudder. Someone once, very seriously, asked early-twentieth-century British writer G. K. Chesterton, "If you were stranded on an island and could have just one book, what would it be?" Instead of the very spiritual or literary-minded answer expected, Chesterton replied, "Why, *A Practical Guide to Shipbuilding*, of course!"[4]

The Bible is a book on life building, written for us as we sojourn on this planet. Interestingly, it also tells us that the rudder and sail remain in God's control and that we enter the high seas with the understanding that we must trust him. If you do not have the mind of faith, then you will fall into repeated peril—and God will get the blame. A life of simple trust is a blessed life, and it sees beyond any impediment through the mind committed to God's way.

Finding the Road

Whenever the apostle Paul writes about having the mind of Christ, his words almost always reference our Lord's sacrifice. In Philippians, he tells us that Jesus denied himself all the prerogatives of divine power in order to become as one of us (see Philippians 2:5–8). In Romans, he challenges us to present our bodies a living sacrifice, which is part and parcel of the renewing of our minds (see Romans 12:1–2). I would like to take us to the third step—a step that involves the *cross*—to fully grasp what this means.

In South American towns and cities you often see a tall statue of Christ standing atop the highest hill (for example, the "Christ the Redeemer" statue in Rio de Janeiro, Brazil). These statues stand there for two reasons: for "protection" from the highest vantage point, and because Christ sees over the hill as no one else can.

The hill of Calvary lies at the very center point of the gospel. All the suffering of the world converged there in that single act of sacrifice when the One without sin took the penalty of our sin and accepted the ultimate in suffering—separation from his Father—so that we might be drawn near to him. That was the lowest point of the incarnate Christ—to be separated from the Father while still in the center of the Father's will. There the threads converged in a pattern that seemed so disparate from the world's point of view, yet they supplied the crimson threads of our restoration to God.

I recall a student at a university campus asking me once why there had to be "all that blood and stuff" in the sacrifice of Jesus. Why couldn't God just make a simple pronouncement of forgiveness to all who sought it—a kind of blanket amnesty? This is precisely the way we look at suffering. Why does it have to be actual? Why not just have it as an idea? Such a wish, however, misses the very nature of reality by not seeing the physical side of the spiritual reality to which God points us.

A few years ago, I held some meetings in Scotland, accompanied by my wife and son and my colleague Stuart and his wife. Stuart is from Scotland, and I often joke with him about needing an interpreter when he speaks English. We toured the country together, and I asked if we could visit Glencoe. Those who are not familiar with the story of Glencoe will wonder what makes this area a tourist attraction. To this day, the region carries the terrible memory of the slaughter of the clan of MacDonald on February 13, 1692, at the hands of the Campbells.

The Campbells came to Glencoe posing as friends. The MacDonald clan showed them great hospitality, unaware that the Campbells came on a mission from the English king to wipe out their clan. In the dead of night, while their hosts slept, the

Campbells put their scheme to work. A song titled "The Massacre of Glencoe" immortalizes the story:

> Chorus: *Oh, cruel is the snow that sweeps Glencoe*
> *and covers the graves o' Donald.*
> *Oh, cruel was the foe that raped Glencoe*
> *and murdered the house o' MacDonald.*
>
> *They came in a blizzard, we offered them heat,*
> *a roof o'er their heads, dry shoes for their feet.*
> *We wined them and dined them, they ate of our meat*
> *and they slept in the house o' MacDonald.* Chorus
>
> *They came from Fort William with murder in mind.*
> *The Campbells had orders King William had signed.*
> *"Put all to the sword," these words underlined,*
> *and leave none alive called MacDonald.* Chorus
>
> *They came in the night while the men were asleep,*
> *this band of Argyles, through snow soft and deep.*
> *Like murdering foxes among helpless sheep,*
> *they slaughtered the house o' MacDonald.* Chorus
>
> *Some died in their beds at the hand of the foe.*
> *Some fled in the night and were lost in the snow.*
> *Some lived to accuse him who struck the first blow,*
> *but gone was the house o' MacDonald.* Chorus[5]

Three hundred years after it happened, this infamous incident continues to be remembered as though it had taken place yesterday. As you enter the Glencoe area, a lone piper slowly paces back and forth, playing the haunting melody. The tragic story and mournful song always leave me heavyhearted. But here's what I noticed: when Stuart talked about the massacre of Glencoe, with the sounds of the bagpipe behind him, his Scottish accent and the woeful groans of that distinctively Scottish instrument amid the ruins of the place where it all happened almost made me feel that I had been there when it occurred.

Carry it one step further. What if one of the victims of the massacre of Glencoe had left behind a tape recording, allowing us to hear the incident in actual terms, not just in memorialized ones? That is how reality must be seen. If we cannot be there, we must see it through the eyes of one who carries the sound and strains of what happened.

If a thick accent, the precise historical location, and somber music can put the reality within reach, even though we remain separated by three centuries, how much more can we understand suffering when we see it through the eyes of the One who defines good and evil, comfort and suffering, and who went to the cross to deal with it? Is this not the only way we can understand and cope with our own suffering? We must see the world of pain through the eyes of Jesus, who best understands it not merely as pain but as brokenness and separation. In the solitude of reflection, the heart and the mind come together to think of the cross. It is here that I think the hymnwriter has something very practical to tell us:

> I sometimes think about the cross
> And shut my eyes and try to see
> The cruel nails and crown of thorns
> And Jesus crucified for me.
> But even could I see him die,
> I could but see a little part
> Of that great love, which, like a fire,
> Is always burning in his heart.[6]

In his own inimitable way, Malcolm Muggeridge says it so powerfully:

Every now and then, I would catch a glimpse of a cross—not necessarily a crucifix; Maybe two pieces of wood accidentally nailed together, on a telegraph pole, for instance—and suddenly my heart would stand still. In an instinctive, intuitive way I understood that something more important, more tumultuous, more passionate, was at issue than our good causes, however admirable they might be.

It was an obsessive interest ... this symbol which was considered to be derisory in my home, was yet also the focus of inconceivable hopes and desires.

As I remember this, a sense of my own failure lies leadenly upon me. I should have worn it over my heart; carried it, a precious standard, never to be wrested out of my hands; even though I fell, still borne aloft. It should have been my cult, my uniform, my language, my life. I shall have no excuse; I can't say I didn't know. I knew from the beginning, and turned away.[7]

The love of God shows us that God alone bridges the distance between him and us, enabling us to see this world through Calvary. If you don't see it that way, then you will never see it his way—and the threads of the masterpiece he is weaving of your life will always pull away from the design.

The Most Important Thread

Once you take these three steps—allow God to make your heart tender, strengthen your mind through faith, and make the cross the aortic nerve of your life—the result follows. You see God's pattern in you and become the instrument of consolation for those who hurt.

This is precisely what Paul meant when he said, "I want to know Christ and the power of his resurrection and the fellowship of sharing in his sufferings, becoming like him in his death, and so, somehow, to attain to the resurrection from the dead" (Philippians 3:10–11). Note the interesting sequence in which Paul puts his knowledge of Jesus. He came to know Christ chronologically by seeing Christ's resurrection power *before* his crucifixion purpose. All of the other disciples followed the more logical sequence—from the cross to the resurrection. Paul went the opposite way—from the resurrection to the cross. The resurrection displayed God's power, while the cross looked like weakness. God asked Paul, in effect, to take a regressive journey, because without the cross there is no resurrection. That is why Paul himself made the cross the core of his message.

It does not surprise me that the book of Psalms is the most read and most preached-from book in the Bible. In this book we read of every anguish the human heart has ever felt, every emotion that ever surged through the human breast, every betrayal ever experienced on the human scene, every foible and sin ever expressed by the human will. All of this comes to us primarily through David, a man who experienced it all and who reminds us that even if we walk through the valley of death, God's staff and rod will protect and comfort.

Someone once elaborated on each line of the well-known and much-loved Psalm 23:

> *The Lord is my Shepherd—that's relationship!*
> *I shall not be in want—that's supply!*
> *He makes me lie down in green pastures—that's rest!*
> *He leads me beside quiet waters—that's refreshment!*
> *He restores my soul—that's healing!*
> *He guides me in the paths of righteousness—that's guidance!*
> *For His name's sake—that's purpose!*
> *Even though I walk through the valley of the shadow of death—*
>   *that's testing!*
> *I will fear no evil—that's protection!*
> *For you are with me—that's faithfulness!*
> *Your rod and the staff, they comfort me—that's discipline!*
> *You prepare a table before me in the presence of my enemies—*
>   *that's hope!*

You anoint my head with oil—that's consecration!
My cup overflows—that's abundance!
Surely goodness and love will follow me all the days of my life—
   that's blessing!
And I will dwell in the house of the Lord—that's security!
Forever—that's eternity!

AUTHOR OF ELABORATED MATERIAL UNKNOWN

This broad but specific, sweeping but individual, assurance came from the pen of a man after God's own heart. Only when you see this pattern for yourself can you see the breadth of God's care for the cosmic scene *and* his personal care for your life. The single most important thread in working through your disappointments is that your heart and mind ponder and grasp what the cross of Jesus Christ is all about. Either your heart and mind will be shaped by that reality or they will be misshapen by false utopias. There is no pattern without the cross. There is no Good News without it. That is what the gospel is all about.

CHAPTER 3

Your Calling Matters

AN OLD SUPERSTITION FROM THE EAST ENCOURAGES PARENTS TO predict their child's future. Folk wisdom suggests that while the child is still a toddler, the parent should place on a table, within the child's reach, a bottle of wine, some money, and a Bible. If the little one walks up to the table and picks up the Bible, he will follow a spiritual vocation, possibly the priesthood. If he picks up the bottle of wine, then hedonism is in the cards. If he picks up the money, he will probably become a businessperson or an entrepreneur.

The story is told of a new father, eager to plan for his son's future, who administered the test. He carefully positioned the three objects on the coffee table, watching eagerly what the little boy would do with them. The little guy walked up to the table, surveyed everything, and slowly reached out his hand for the Bible. Then he paused and picked up the money as well, placing it in the Bible. Finally he tucked the Bible under one arm, took the bottle of wine in the other hand, and toddled off with all three, struggling to maintain his balance. The little boy's grandfather stood over to the side, silently watching the whole scene unfold. When he saw the dismay on his own son's face, he said, "This is bad news. He's going to become a politician."

We chuckle at a story like this because we tend to be quite skeptical about the men and women who inhabit the world of politics. We imagine them playing games with power, sometimes moralizing about other people's foibles and sometimes caught in duplicitous relationships themselves—and always, of course, with an eye on financial gain. But it's really not fair to the politician, because too often the so-called spiritually minded, as well as the business-minded, have tried the same ploys and managed to fool the masses in similar ways.

The Search for Success

We all seek success, eager to grab whatever we can along the way. Just look at the sections in our bookstores that promote resources about motivation and career selection, and you'll find all the advice you need on how to find that specific purpose for which you are distinctly wired. We all seem to want to be number one, as if that is the only way we can measure our success (or lack of it). It seems to be the hot topic of today.

I think of the comical words of a certain university president, who supposedly said, "What we need is a university the football team can be proud of." Excelling in sports is an extraordinary accomplishment and only the best survive. A professional athlete or ball player has a genius all his or her own and it is to be admired. But we make a huge mistake in taking our cue from competitive sports and applying the guidelines that govern success in sports to how we measure success in other areas of life. Remember the words of the legendary football coach that "there is no room for second place"? There was "only one place in my game," he said, "and that's first place. There is a second place bowl game, but it is a game for losers played by losers. It is and always has been an American zeal to be first in anything we do, and to win, and to win, and to win."[1]

As marvelous as it all sounds, this quote is laden with seductive half-truths packaged to impart some kind of recipe for bringing the trophy home. Although it would be nice if all of us could be number one, it just is not possible or realistic. Somebody has to be number two—and number three and four, and on down the line. That doesn't make them losers. Not everyone can be the general in the army. Sadly, the drive to become number one is often the very thing that ultimately destroys a person. It simply cannot deliver the fulfillment we seek. Story after story bears this out.

Some time ago, I read about former New York Mets pitcher Dwight Gooden. Even as I write, he is serving a prison term for parole violation following a cocaine offense. Gooden was rookie of the year in 1984 and a Cy Young award winner in 1985. What more could a Major League pitcher want in his first two years on the mound? He had one more goal. In 1986 the Mets won the World Series in a spectacular, come-from-behind win over the Red Sox. Gooden was a member of that team. The championship capped a storybook sequence of his first three years in the majors.

Now in prison, Gooden looks back on that championship year with a broken heart and shattered dreams. He remembers not his feelings of ecstasy in becoming a "world champion," but that it was then that he began his flirtation with cocaine. From that time on, his career spiraled down until it had vanished.

Accomplishment and dream careers do not necessarily lead to happiness. Making it to number one really means knowing where God wants you to be and serving him there with your best efforts. The goal, then, is to find the threads God has in place for you and to follow his plan for you with excellence.

Attainment and Contentment

We often find out too late in life that attaining a pursuit and finding fulfillment are not necessarily the same thing. It is surely possible to find meaning without achieving extraordinary success. Many people do. Immense success does not always bring meaning or fulfillment. For some, finding their calling does mean success, but often this success comes after repeated failures. And sometimes it takes an entire lifetime to recognize God's calling.

I think of two contrasting individuals. One is little known on this side of the Atlantic, while the other is known through his poetry, made famous long after his death. The first is John Howard, a contemporary of John Wesley, Charles Wesley, George Whitefield, and William Carey. Since he worked behind the scenes, his name did not have as high a profile as theirs.

In 1775, when he was just twenty-nine years old, Howard lost his wife. As he sat by her body, heartbroken over her death, he heard that a catastrophic earthquake had struck Lisbon, Portugal, and that tens of thousands of people had died. Even today, that earthquake is ranked as one of the most devastating in history. Survivors sent out an urgent call for help worldwide, and Howard made the commitment that, despite his personal grief, he would take the next boat to Lisbon and provide whatever help he could. He booked himself on the English ship *Hanover*, but en route a French mercenary vessel seized the ship (England and France were at war at the time). Along with others, Howard was thrown into a dungeon, where he was deprived of food, water, and even sunlight. The hellish conditions in the jail utterly shocked him. One need only read of the conditions in a history book to grasp the cruelty of it all, a situation true all across England and Europe. The writer of *A Short History of the English People* described the English prison system as "a perfect chaos of cruelty."

In that brief incarceration, Howard's soul awakened to the horrible conditions in European prisons and to the degradation and abuse inflicted on human beings for petty crimes. Howard found one man who had died after rotting in prison for ten years. His crime? He owed a tradesman a mere seven pounds. Howard's heart could no longer endure the abuse without trying to change his world. Interestingly enough, years before, when he was only twenty-four, he had written these words in his journal:

Lord, I believe; help Thou mine unbelief! Here, on this sacred day, in the dust before the eternal God, I cast my guilty and polluted soul on the sovereign mercy of the Redeemer. Oh, compassionate and divine Lord, save me from the dreadful guilt and power of sin, and accept my solemn, free, and unreserved surrender! Look upon me, a repenting, returning prodigal! Thus, O Lord God, am I humbly bold to covenant with Thee! Ratify and confirm it, and make me the everlasting monument of Thy mercy, Glory to God—Father, Son, and Holy Ghost—for ever and ever. Amen and Amen.[2]

No one, perhaps especially Howard himself, could have guessed what would happen in his soul during those few short hours in prison in answer to this prayer. In the years to come, he would stand before parliaments and rulers and lawmakers until he changed the course of history. In Europe, nation after nation introduced prison reform bills. His impact was felt in the Bastille, the French galleys, the prisons of the Spanish Inquisition and in the lazarettos of Turkey. As a tribute to his service, his statue was the first to be placed in St. Paul's Cathedral in London. When you read his journal, you see notation after notation of his desire that his name not be exalted but that his cause never be forgotten. He wanted to be a monument to God's mercy. Reading about a life such as his makes any desire on our part to be number one, frankly, pathetic. John Howard found his calling. And what led him to it? A death, a terrible earthquake, a war, and the putrid jail of a mercenary vessel.

The other man was Francis Thompson, a genius with no aptitude for the academy. His father wanted him to become a medical doctor. But every time Francis tried to gain entrance into Oxford University, he failed. His repeated failures only sent him into the cavern of his own soul, where he dreamed poetry, wrote it down, and sent it to newspaper editors. During this time of his desert wanderings, he hung about Charing Cross with the losers and the lost, wrapping himself in a dirty raincoat to sleep along with the homeless beside the river Thames. But Thompson's soul stirred with the gift within him. Today when you read "The Hound of Heaven" and his other brilliant works, you cannot but thank God for Thompson's repeated failed attempts at medicine. To me, two stanzas of his great masterpiece "The Kingdom of God" sum up his life:

> *But (when so sad, thou canst not sadder)*
> *Cry,—and upon thy so sore loss*
> *Shall shine the traffic of Jacob's ladder,*
> *Pitched betwixt Heaven and Charing Cross.*
>
> *Yea, in the night, my Soul, my daughter,*
> *Cry,—clinging Heaven by the hems;*
> *And lo, Christ walking on the water*
> *Not of Gennesareth, but Thames!*[3]

What genius inspired these lines! No, the goal is really not to be number one, nor is it to follow the dreams of others. God, in his extraordinary way, can bring failure to you or cast you into prison in order to help you find your true calling.

What Is a Calling?

A calling is simply God's shaping of your burden and beckoning you to your service to him in the place and pursuit of his choosing. Finding your home in your service to Christ is key to noticing the threads designed just for you. It gives you that hand-in-glove sensation and provides the security of knowing that you are utilizing your gifts and your will to God's ends first, not for yours. When your will becomes aligned with God's will, his calling upon you has found its home.

The Bible clearly lays down the starting point for this—and it is not terribly hard to discern. Whenever someone exercises leadership in the Bible, you notice the extraordinary lengths to which God goes in his pronouncement of the character and the vision of the person pursuing the call: "he did what was right in the eyes of the LORD" (see, for example, 2 Kings 14:3; 15:3, 34); "he did evil in the eyes of the LORD" (see, for example, 2 Kings 13:2, 11; 14:24). One of these two lines summarizes years and years of a life.

A call may not necessarily feel attractive to you, but it will tug on your soul in an inescapable way, no matter how high the cost of following it may be. We more loosely refer to it as "God's call." Yes, it is his beckoning; but it is more. It is God's vital purpose in positioning you in life and giving you the vocation and context of your call to serve him with a total commitment to do the job well.

I have met businessmen who described their dream of a preaching ministry, while few are the preachers who have not flirted with the idea of launching out into business. My own background is hotel management, and I have always dreamed of owning a restaurant. But that will forever remain in the "if I had two lives to live" category. I still work up recipes in my mind and accompaniments for main courses and sauces to tantalize the taste buds. But it was not to be. My second dream was to play professional cricket. To this very day, that dream haunts me, though the possibility has completely evaporated—unless, of course, some team were looking for a mate to play against their grandchildren. God clearly called me into the preaching and teaching ministry, principally in hostile arenas. An odd call for a shy individual, I would think! But God does it his way.

God trained Moses in a palace to use him in a desert. He trained Joseph in a desert to use him in a palace. Some come through winding paths, some through the nicely paved road of privileged birth or influential friends. Others come through the visitation of circumstances with wanderings and sudden signposts. Finding one's calling is one of the greatest challenges in life, especially when one has gifts that fan out in many directions.

Hindsight

I said earlier that one often sees a call only in retrospect. This too, strangely, is by God's design. When God called the Israelites out of Egypt, he made an astounding statement. Remember the intense dialogue between a reluctant Moses and a beckoning God in Exodus 3? Moses finally says in exasperation, "But how do I know it is you who is calling us?" This audacious challenge came even after supernatural events had provided clear evidence of God's involvement in this plan. Who would need more than a burning bush that is engulfed by flames but is not consumed, or an audible voice that issues a call? These are not routine daily events.

To Moses' question, God makes a remarkable reply: "After you have entered the land, you will know that it is I who has called you" (see Exodus 3:12). I can just see Moses' face. He probably wanted to say, "Thanks a lot, but by then it'll be too late to find out if it isn't you calling." As much as that retrospective look troubles us, however, it makes for a fascinating confirmation that without God, the thing never would have happened.

God reinforces his call as we respond to his nod. If we were to see the final design in prospect, we would find ourselves acting on the basis of self-love and pragmatism—and then, who would need faith? God often reinforces our faith *after* we trust him, not before.

Sometimes the melodrama of someone else's call colors our own expectations of a call. We've all read of some dramatic incident in someone's life that causes us to recognize God's sovereign intervention behind the scenes in some critical incident in our own lives. I think of a young British politician who, when visiting Washington, D.C., was hit by a car while crossing the road. The accident should have permanently disabled him, if not taken his life. In his own words, he should have been squashed beyond recognition.[4] Thankfully, neither happened. Those who were there saw it as the fortunate preservation of a single life, nothing more. But history showed differently. We can only ponder what the future of our planet might have looked like had Winston Churchill's life not been spared that day. To stop a Hitler, it took a Churchill.

The Bible is full of stories about incredible leaders rescued in very dramatic settings—Moses, Paul, Daniel, and others. The same is true in church history: think of John Wesley, Blaise Pascal, and countless others. But we must recognize that it does not always happen that way, and God can call us by slow, encouraging methods as well as by dramatic ones. The real challenge is to ponder how we come to terms with God's sovereign working and how we respond to his plan and calling. This is where our hopes and dreams often become confused with our capacities and our calling. How do we get to the place that God has for us?

Signposts along the Way

Fortunately, the Christian walk is not a clueless journey that begins with conversion and ends with heaven, while we mark time in between. No, God has designed us to work for his honor.

One of the greatest books ever written, a book that has sold more copies than any other book except the Bible, is John Bunyan's *Pilgrim's Progress*. Ironically, Bunyan spent most of his life mending pots and pans, but we find his greater workmanship in this immortal book that tells how God works in us, shaping and molding us for the journey we undertake as we follow him.

Pilgrim's Progress is an allegory. A character named Christian starts his journey bearing his burden on his back. He experiences all the vicissitudes of life, struggling and battling until he ultimately ends up in the Celestial City. Bunyan's rare genius allows him to describe the struggles we all face before we get to that glorious destination. He simply could not have penned this book without having personally undergone all the tumult that he so accurately portrays in his description of the Christian walk.

He tells us with great insight how the pilgrim, Christian, attired in rags and weighed down by his burden, reaches a hill, where he encounters the cross. He is searching for the Celestial City but discovers one cannot enter the city without going by way of the cross. As he looks up at the cross, he falls to his knees and the burden falls off his back. But this is not the end of the story! He is still at the beginning of his journey. Burdens are not just lifted at the cross; some new ones are added to give direction to our call.

After Christian loses his burden of guilt and sin, three "Shining Ones" greet him. The first of these three is the Angel of the Dawn, who greets him with the words, "Thy sins be forgiven thee." The second, the Angel of the Daylight, strips him of his rags and gives him a new set of clothes. The third, the Angel of the Dusk, points the way for Christian to walk toward the gate of the Celestial City.[5] This third angel puts a mark on his forehead and then gives him a scroll—a map to guide him on his way. The first angel meets his spiritual need; the second addresses his physical needs; and the third engages his intellectual needs and gives him the tools to instruct him along the journey.

The Christian's walk involves all three areas of life—the spiritual, the practical, and the logical—which are not mutually exclusive. God is an immensely practical being who also guides us with reason and wisdom. Let us see how the threads of *your* hopes, *your* dreams, and *your* calling come into place spiritually, practically, and intellectually.

An Incorruptible Treasure

For just a moment, I want to move from the image of fabric and thread to the metaphor of a precious stone. The Bible often refers to our salvation in gemological terms. The prophet refers to God's people as "jewels in a crown" (Zechariah 9:16). The Bible describes us as those who undergo trials and are tested so as to be refined like gold in a furnace (see Job 23:10; Isaiah 48:10; 1 Peter 1:6–7). Jesus speaks of the kingdom of God as the pearl "of great value" (see Matthew 13:45–46). We have a great inheritance and a precious calling.

In his first letter, the apostle Peter, an ordinary fisherman, writes of our inheritance from God (1 Peter 1:4). He uses three Greek words (*aphtharton, amianton,* and *amaranton*) to describe a treasure that is incorruptible and undefiled and that does not fade away. This is what we are seeking—a life and a calling that do not get corrupted along the journey, that cannot be defiled by earthly distractions, and that will not grow dim or dull with time. This treasure is beyond corruption, beyond decay, and beyond tarnishing.

It takes multiple skills and trained specialists to take a diamond in the rough and produce the multifaceted, brilliant stone that eventually adorns someone's hand. The stages of the refining of the diamond suggest many applications for our own lives. The most important is to know that God shapes the precious life he saves and does so for a special purpose. A new burden begins, a new impetus lodges in the heart. A new purpose for doing what you do steadies that call. The pattern starts to unfold — a pattern for which God has been shaping you as he takes you through a lifelong pursuit and to a treasured fulfillment of serving him well.

The Big Picture

Every calling that honors God's purpose for life in general is a sacred call. We noticed this in the prayer of John Howard (cited on page 57), prayed long before he responded to the specifics of that call. It is often in this waiting that we get lost and our vision becomes blurred.

God calls us "a kingdom of priests" (1 Peter 2:9 NLT). This status, in itself, positions us for the sacred. Sadly, the church has historically been a key culprit in destroying this privilege for the masses. This blunder has resulted in great cost to the church in her role in history and in society. She erred by dividing callings into false hierarchies, and we are still dealing with the problems that resulted.

Some years ago, I walked through the home of Martin Luther the Reformer in Wittenberg, Germany. I marveled at some of the documents of the church of his day, which I saw on display there, including one referring to a statement issued by the papacy that decreed that if someone's mother suffered in purgatory, at the exact moment the person purchased an indulgence, the mother would immediately be moved into heaven.

Can you see how corrupt the church became when it started to make a profitable business out of selling salvation? The practice had become an abuse of the uninformed, operated as a monopoly by those who thought they alone served as priests — and Luther railed against it. He did not demand the abolition of the priesthood but rather fought for the abolition of the laity.

Because we are all priests before God, there is no such distinction as "secular or sacred." In fact, the opposite of sacred is not secular; the opposite of sacred is profane. In short, *no* follower of Christ does secular work. We all have a sacred calling.

Seeking our particular call, we might well ask, "Are we all dreamers? Are we all designed to hope and plan?" In specific moments in history, God has raised up particular individuals with a momentous call, people such as the pharaoh of the exodus, David, Jeremiah, Daniel, Esther, Paul, and many others. And though we may not know the names of many, many more, their callings are just as certain and needed.

That truth is what I want us to consider and ponder. If my very ethnicity and my disappointments make up part of God's pattern for my life, then it stands to reason that so does my calling before him. He has intricately woven together my hopes, my dreams, and my vocation. God's plan for each one of us includes the way he has wired our thinking and has prepared whatever it is in our lives that will bring us fulfillment.

The process that takes us from rough-hewn to finely polished has many facets. We all are concerned primarily with the particulars or the end product of our personal shaping, but God first deals with the generalities that provide the backdrop for his specific claim on our lives. God reveals the particulars of our calling against the backdrop of the general call of the believer.

Our First Call

And what is the first call for each one of us? It is to understand God's primary description of who and what we are. All the other accolades that people want to thrust at us are secondary at best. The fact that someone writes, another speaks, still others invest or play sports, is merely the *means* to express the greater end.

Some time ago, I attended a Bible study session with some sports professionals. The speaker that morning challenged the players to leave a legacy they could be proud of. He began by asking them how many knew the name of their great-grandfather. A handful of hands went up. Then he asked how many of them knew where their great-grandfather was buried. Most of the hands stayed down. With each more specific question, fewer hands went up. He then made his point: "Each one of us is just three to four generations away from extinction." Silence gripped the room. How sobering to think that, just a few generations down the family tree, no one would even know I had ever existed! Then the speaker challenged these men about the legacy they would leave behind. One after another, the players responded.

But then one said, "Really, I don't care whether or not my great-great-grandson or great-granddaughter knows that I played ball professionally. It really doesn't matter that much. I just want them to know the God I served and loved." The words came from the heart, and for a moment, in the silence, we all knew the truth of both thoughts.

Our devotion to God's call and to his claim on our lives provides the groundwork of all that ultimately matters. Words like those of the professional ballplayer are all the more profound, because many of our youth consider his calling a dream. But the greatest dream of all is to know God and to know what he has intended for your life. So the conclusion of the matter is this: the general is the foundation, and the particular is the structure that is built on it.

A Temple for God

The Bible gives the blueprint for this foundation in a metaphorical description of every follower of Jesus Christ. The apostle Paul refers to us as the temple in which God lives (see

1 Corinthians 3:16–17; 6:19; 2 Corinthians 6:16; Ephesians 2:21–22). The adornment of the temple—the colors, precious stones, gold, and ornaments—was incidental to the reason for the temple. It existed as a dwelling place for God.

That is the starting point for any call. One simply cannot mix the profane with the sacred. To know that I am God's temple is to know that my very being is a sacred expression. If I am a doctor, can I make decisions that desacralize life? If I am a publisher, can I distribute profane material? If I am an athlete, can I cheat on the rules? If I am in ministry, can I use manipulative methods to support myself? The answer to all of these is the same: "Absolutely not!" The ends can never justify the means. The means must justify themselves. This makes living as a Christian difficult because we often feel tempted to compromise our foundational beliefs in order to attain some pragmatic end.

A few miles from where I live, a business promotes itself as an "adult toy and amusement center." It is really none of the above. It is not for adults; it principally caters to men who have never grown up morally. It does not sell something to toy with; sexuality is sacred, and using it for amusement brings diminishing returns. It is not a center; it distorts life's central point.

The ironic thing about the owner is that in an interview with the media, he proclaimed his Christian faith. He sees nothing wrong with the stuff he peddles. The Bible, to the contrary, says that a person like this—one who destroys lives—would be better off to have a millstone hung about his neck and be thrown into the sea than to fall into God's hands (see Matthew 18:6). He has lost life's central feature, which alone can determine all other calls.

The book of Exodus powerfully expounds the purpose of our redemption and the pattern for our service. God himself dictates the blueprint for the tabernacle, which served as the precursor to the temple. He calls Moses to go up on the mountain and keeps him there for six days while a cloud envelops the mountain. Then, for the next thirty-four days, God proceeds to give Moses every particular for the building and function of the tabernacle—from what goes where to who builds what—in extensive and precise detail.

Seriously, we might ask whether God really needed to do this. Couldn't he just have trusted his builders to carry out the task? But as he begins his instructions, he says, "Have them make a sanctuary for me, and I will dwell among them. Make this tabernacle and all its furnishings exactly like the pattern I will show you" (Exodus 25:8–9). At the end of God's instructions, he says, "There I will meet you and speak to you; ... and the place will be consecrated by my glory" (Exodus 29:42–43). The passage speaks of three things: God's presence, his voice, and the consecration of the structure for his glory—the three "shining ones" once more, albeit in different words.

In terms of Jesus' call on each of us, *we* are now that tabernacle and the dwelling place of God, a truth that is utterly unique and distinctive from all other faiths. The Muslim must face Mecca while he prays. In any hotel in the Middle East you can see the arrows pointing toward Mecca. It is all a compulsory ceremony and leads to the manipulating of millions of minds. In temples of other religions, one must abide by certain ceremonies and priestly roles deemed compulsory for the purpose of worship.

But the pilgrim who has seen his burden roll away at the cross now becomes the temple, and thus communion with God becomes personal and near. *That* is the backdrop of all of our callings.

The doctor reveres the patient for the same reason a ballplayer takes care of his physique. The particulars of their call differ because the site of their sanctuary differs. But the privilege of individual and equal access to God—anytime, anywhere—remains the same. That is what makes their calling equally sacred. You and I are temples. What a divine metaphor to position our call! One simply does not profane the temple.

The Particular Thread

Now that we have established the body as sacred, we can deal with the capacities of the mind and with individual skills and gifts. You will have no trouble imagining what to do with your life if you can do only one thing. But what about the person who is capable of fulfilling many vocations and of doing them all well?

One of the great heroes of the Christian faith in the past few centuries was Robert Murray McCheyne. Most people with even a scant knowledge of church history will recognize his name. The equally famed Andrew Bonar penned his life story in a book called *The Secret of Robert Murray McCheyne*, and that biography had a profound impact on my life as a young Christian.

McCheyne served as pastor of St. Peter's in Dundee, Scotland when, at age twenty-nine, he died while yet in the fresh bloom of his ministry. I consider him to have been one of the most gifted individuals ever to enter the call of the ministry. He had a firm grip on many languages, including Latin, Hebrew, and Greek. He was a gifted musician who was skilled in many instruments. As a scholar he had particular authority in geology and natural history. He was also an artist, a poet, and a gifted singer. He excelled in athletics, and, in fact, a pole-vaulting injury may have hastened his death. So much was wrapped into one man.

Yet the greatest happening in his church took place during his absence. He had been quite unwell for some time and took a sabbatical to Palestine and Eastern Europe for rest. A young W. C. Burns took charge of the pulpit during McCheyne's absence, and a historic revival broke out in St. Peter's, spreading throughout all of Scotland. When McCheyne heard reports from his beloved homeland and from the church so dear to his heart, he longed to at least have an opportunity to witness something of what was happening. He returned home and looked forward to joining his voice to the marvelous thing God was doing in and through St. Peter's. It shocked him to see the crowd that had gathered to hear him speak, as it overflowed into every available room in the building. At the young age of twenty-six, he saw the wondrous move of God—and a short three years later, the Lord called him home. His role in the revival occurred behind the scenes, as a paver of the way for it all to happen. How did he know his calling and recognize its impact? In Bonar's biography we find several clues. I will underscore three in particular.

First, he had a devout prayer life. One simply cannot know one's call without coming near to God in prayer.

One story describes how a young clergyman from England visited St. Peter's to learn more about McCheyne. The caretaker of the building showed him around, and when the clergyman asked about McCheyne's secret, the caretaker replied, "Sit down here," as he pointed to McCheyne's chair. "Now put your elbows on the table; now put your face in your hands—now let the tears flow."

Then he took the visitor to the pulpit from which McCheyne had preached. "Put your elbows on the pulpit; now put your face in your hands—now let the tears flow."

It was as simple and as profound as that. McCheyne felt content to see the revival break out under another man's preaching because he had prayed for that revival. No, he didn't occupy the number one spot when the revival came; but he was still the winner. He had focused his prayers on this revival, and God had answered those prayers.

I do not believe that one can earnestly seek and find the priceless treasure of God's call without a devout prayer life. Each of us is the temple of the Lord, and it was the Lord who said, "My house will be called a house of prayer" (Isaiah 56:7).

That is where God speaks. The purpose of prayer and of God's call in your life is not to make you number one in the world's eyes, but to make him number one in your life. His calling is perfect, and he has a specific place for each one. Every member of the body has a particular role, and we find our fulfillment in filling that role.

This leads to the second significant clue—the willingness to be outshone while shining for God. Humility is the touchstone of serving God. Many fail in the pulpit because of failure in this area. We hear so much these days about "bigger churches" and "bigger church events" and "greater attendance." We hear very little about being smaller in our own self-estimate.

F. W. Boreham wrote two essays that greatly helped me clarify my thinking about a divine call—"The Poppies in the Corn" and "The Carpenter Encouraged the Goldsmith." Both make the same point but in a different way. In his essay on poppies, Boreham writes:

> There is a very lovable thing about the poppies in the corn that I can sufficiently admire. The poppies never belittle the corn. They glorify it. You think not less but the more of the corn because of the presence of the poppies. At a rose show one particularly radiant blossom puts to shame all the surrounding roses. They are beggared by comparison. That is because a show is all artificiality and affectation. Nature never humiliates her more modest children in that ridiculous way. As you watch the blood-red poppies tossing in a sea of golden corn, it never occurs to you to institute a comparison. The poppies and the corn seem equally lovely. That is the glory of true greatness.
>
> *A commonplace life, we say and we sigh,*
> *But why do we sigh as we say?*
> *The commonplace sun in the commonplace sky*
> *Makes up the commonplace day.*

The moon and the stars are commonplace things,
And the flower that blooms and the bird that sings;
But dark were the world and sad our lot,
If the flowers failed and the sun shone not.
And God who studies each separate soul
Out of commonplace lives makes His beautiful whole.[6]

Yours may seem to be a "commonplace" call, but there is no such thing in God's eyes. The rose or the poppy simply cannot steal the show. Without the soil and the sun and the nurture and the care, the rose or the poppy could never grow. "Lesser" powers behind the scene prop up the majestic. And as for the corn, it has a country beauty all its own as its golden heads sway in the breeze. Its nourishment feeds the one who tends the soil where the rose blooms. The flower and the cactus each has its own majesty.

In his other essay, "The Carpenter Encouraged the Gold-smith" (the phrase is borrowed from the prophet Isaiah), Boreham reminds us of two distinctive trades. The carpenter operates on wood, the goldsmith on gold. One uses a hammer, a saw, nails, and chisels; the other works with fine instruments. You might think the goldsmith would inspire the carpenter, but it's the other way around, according to Isaiah 41:7 (KJV): "The carpenter encouraged the goldsmith."

The simple and the rough-and-tumble can win the sophisti-cated. A servant who nursed Charles Wesley as he lay critically ill while in his thirties won him to the Lord. Another servant won the famed Lord Shaftesbury to the Savior. Both worked as carpenters pleased to be among those who encouraged gold-smiths. Someone who stands under the bright lights of history will never, in God's eyes, outshine the humble attractiveness of the one who humbly serves God.

The preparation for the call through prayer and the attitude of living out the call in humility, take us to the final step: the role that godly people played in McCheyne's life, as they do in yours and mine as well. This important clue to knowing God's call—making certain that you stay close to those who walk closely with God—often gets missed. At my father-in-law's funeral, his doctor spoke about the kind of man he was and commented that he had chosen his mentors and his heroes at a young age. When you put your trust in godly men and women, you never walk alone.

In the early days of my ministry, I received an invitation to preach in a church whose pastor was a highly successful, godly man. I asked him how he would know when he had finished his work in that particular place. He smiled and said, "It is already set in place now. I have told my elders that I will continue to serve here as long as my service for God remains fruitful. When the elders of the church are unanimously certain that the time has come for me to move on, I have asked them to let me know, and within twenty-four hours they will have my resignation."

"That's quite a gamble you have taken," I said.

"I'm trusting the Lord to lead me this way," he responded, "because I am not always sure that my motives are not colored as well." I nodded.

About twelve years later, I met him in another setting where he was speaking. "When did you leave that pastorate?" I asked.

He gave me the date and said, "Two of the elders came to me one day, representing the board, and said that they wondered if my time of service there should be coming to an end. By sunset the next day, I had turned in my resignation. There were many tears, but there was much more to celebrate, and I moved on."

On a completely different level, a professional soccer player once told me that in a clutch match he had been asked to replace the star player, who in a previous game had not performed well. As it happened, the young rising star, stepping in to take the place of the veteran, scored the winning goal. From then on, the veteran player's career began to wane because he could not handle the growing fame of his younger contemporary. That's the difference between being where God wants you to be and always wanting to be number one.

Number One in God's Eyes

A man celebrating his seventieth birthday spoke of a dream he had. In the dream he sat at a table with six other people. He sat alone, while the others grouped themselves in pairs:

At the head table:	the man I am.
Facing me:	the man I used to be, number 1
	the man I used to be, number 2.
On my left:	the man I might have been, number 1;
	the man I might have been, number 2.
On my right:	the man I shall be, number 1;
	the man I shall be, number 2.

In effect, he saw the possibilities of the actual in comparison to the potential. He dealt with the one reality of his present state, even as he faced the many possibilities of the future. That was quite a dream: "We are seven."

Submit to God's design, and be number one in his eyes.

Know that you are God's temple. Bathe your life in prayer. Live out your life in humility of spirit that serves for the right reasons. Seek the counsel and example of godly men and women. Finally, exhibit a commitment to the preeminence of Christ in all things. These are the components of a call. Self-glory, power, sensuality, and the seduction of material gain impede such a call.

God is the author of my call. He has the plan in mind, and I must respond to his nod. Take the thread of wanting to serve wherever he wants you and add it to the mix. The design will thrill you one day.

CHAPTER 4

Your Morality Matters

SOME YEARS AGO, I READ AN ARTICLE IN AN IN-FLIGHT MAGAZINE on the subject of ethics. It began with a provocative story undoubtedly designed to instantly gain the attention of the reader. It worked.

The writer described a man aboard a plane who propositioned a woman sitting next to him for one million dollars. She glared at him but pursued the conversation and began to entertain the possibility of so easily becoming a millionaire. The pair set the time, terms, and conditions. Just before he left the plane, he sputtered, "I—I have to admit, ma'am, I have sort of, ah, led you into a lie. I, um, I really don't have a million dollars. Would you consider the proposition for just—ah, say—ah, ten dollars?"

On the verge of smacking him across the face for such an insult, she snapped back, "What do you think I am?"

"That has already been established," he replied. "Now we're just haggling over the price."

I have to admit that when I read this little anecdote, I felt more disgusted with the man who did the propositioning than with the woman who was propositioned. I sensed something mean-spirited about the man who made the offer. He obviously had set her up for the kill. It seemed like one of those manufactured stories where you start with the endgame in view and move backward to the start.

But as I reflected on the writer's conclusion—namely, that everyone has his or her price—I questioned the assumption. While we all may have a price on some matters, I'm equally certain that there are other matters on which no price is right and no sum of money would cause one to budge. Would a man who truly loved his wife or his daughters sell them for a certain price? I think the answer is an overwhelming "absolutely not!"

But then another thought entered my mind. What does one make of the charge that *God himself* has set up a scheme in human relations where the entire game is fixed? Perhaps Adam and Eve could not have resisted the wiles of the devil; perhaps sooner or later the fall would have ensued. Isn't this the way it sometimes appears? First, it is, "Don't look." Then it is, "Don't touch." At least, that's the way the skeptic frames the scheme. One form of desire or another would soon find the price match, and Adam or Eve would succumb.

The garden may have changed, but the tantalizing trade-offs continue as we barter away our souls. This dreadful moral conflict rages within cultures and communities and within each human heart. What is this moral plan about anyway? How does God demand moral rectitude in the pattern he is weaving for you and me in the vast design of the universe, when it seems both impossible and artificial?

The Systemic Difference

The fundamental difference between a naturalist worldview and a religious worldview is the moral framework. While a naturalist may choose to be a moral person, no compelling rational reason exists why one should not be amoral. Reason simply does not dictate here. Pragmatism may, but reason alone doesn't allow one to defend one way over another. Prominent Canadian atheist Kai Nielson said it well:

> We have not been able to show that reason requires the moral point of view, or that really rational persons unhood-winked by myth or ideology need not be individual ego-ists or classical amoralists. Reason doesn't decide here. The picture I have painted for you is not a pleasant one. Re-flection on it depresses me.... Pure practical reason, even with a good knowledge of the facts, will not take you to morality.[1]

Bertrand Russell admitted that he could not live as though ethical values were simply a matter of personal taste. That's why he found his own views incredible. "I do not know the solu-tion," he concluded.[2] Frederick Nietzsche also said as much: "I, too, have to end up worshipping at the altar where God's name is truth."[3] While we cannot escape the moral "stranglehold" our moral bent puts us into, neither can naturalism explain either the inclination toward morality or the conclusion.

So extreme a problem has this created for the naturalist that some have gone to great lengths to deduce even that there is no such thing as good or evil; all of us merely dance to our DNA. This sits very comfortably with them until they irresistibly raise the question of all the "evil" that religion has engendered.

The debate gains rational grounds in the realm of religion, which is why it is critical to understand the similarities and foundational differences between various religions. In every re-ligion except Christianity, morality is a means of attainment.

In Hinduism, for example, every birth is considered a re-birth, and every rebirth is a means to pay for the previous life's shortcomings. To make up for this obvious debit-and-credit ap-proach, Hinduism established the caste system to justify its fatalistic belief. Karma is systemic to the Hindu belief. You cannot be a Hindu and dismiss the reality of karma.

In Buddhism, while every birth is a rebirth, the intrinsic payback is impersonal because Buddhism has no essential self that exists or survives. Life is a force carried forward through reincarnations, and the day you learn there is no essential self and you quit desiring anything is the day that evil dies and suffering ends for you. The extinguishing of self and desire through a moral walk brings the ultimate victory over your imaginary individuality and your suffering. Karma is intrinsic to Buddhism as well, but there is a different doctrine of self at work. While in Hinduism every birth is a rebirth, in Buddhism every birth is a rebirth of an impersonal karma. Only the best of Buddhist scholars are even qualified to discuss these very intricate ideas.

In Islam, the system of tithing, the tax system, the way women are clothed — all the way to the legal structure and the ultimate punishment reserved for apostasy — express the moral framework in which this religion operates. Even then, heaven is not assured (which, ironically, is sensuous in its experience). Only Allah makes the decision about whether an individual gets rewarded with heaven.

In the early days of Israel's formation, moral imperatives extended to every detail of life. Hundreds of laws covered everything from morals to diet to ceremony.

In short, while moral rectitude differs in its details, it is, nevertheless, a factor in determining future blessing or retribution. For the most part, both theistic and pantheistic religions conveyed that idea.

But for the later Hebrews and, in turn, the Christians, two realities make a crucial systemic and distinguishing difference. First and foremost, God is the author of moral boundaries, not man and not culture. Here, Islam and Judaism find a little common ground, at least as the basis. But there the superficial similarities end because the two differ drastically on the very possibility of ascribing attributes to God, the idea of fellowship with God, the entailments of violating his law, and the prescription for restoration. God is so transcendent in Islam that any analogical reference to him in human terms runs the risk of blasphemy.

The book of Genesis, on the other hand, shows God in close fellowship with his human creation. It also gives numerous possibilities to the first creation, with just one restriction: no eating of the fruit from the tree of the knowledge of good and evil. When Adam and Eve violated that restriction, the second injunction took effect: they were not to eat the fruit from the tree of life. When you look carefully at those two boundaries, one following the other, you understand what is going on. Eating the fruit from the tree of the knowledge of good and evil basically gave humanity the power to redefine everything. God had given language, identification, and reality to humankind. He imparted to humans the power to name the animals. But essential to the created order was a moral framework that the creation was *not* to name or define. This was the prerogative of the Creator, not of the creation. I believe that this is what is at stake here.

Does mankind have a right to define what is good and what is evil? Have you never heard this refrain in culture after culture: "What right does any culture have to dictate to another culture what is good?" Embedded in that charge is always another charge: "The evil things that have happened in your culture deny you the prerogative to dictate to anyone else."

Anyone living at the time and old enough to recall will never forget the outrage of some members of the media when President Ronald Reagan denounced the Soviet Union as an "evil empire," or when President George W. Bush branded three nations as forming an "axis of evil." Ayatollah Khomeini of Iran, in the meantime, remained well within his own comfort zone when he pronounced the United States as a "satanic power," according to the same members of the media.

Such moralizing goes on, always with the same bottom line: "Who gives whom the right to pronounce the other evil?" I have heard this question countless times. The very word "morality" has become a lightning-rod theme. "Who is to say what is good? How audacious that anyone should lay claim to an absolute!" This lies at the core of our entire moral predicament, and it is truly fascinating, isn't it? But we find an interesting twist here, because this selective denial of absolutes in morality does not carry over into the sciences.

The Contradictory Approaches

In his book *Glimpsing the Face of God*, Alister McGrath points out an obvious truth that most miss.[4] He uses the illustration of chemical formulas. Every molecule of water has two atoms of hydrogen and one atom of oxygen. The formula H_2O remains true, no matter what race of people or what gender analyzes it. Can one really say, "It's not fair to oxygen that there are two atoms of hydrogen in water; so to be fair, there should be two atoms of oxygen as well"? You can give two atoms of oxygen, if you want to—but if you drink it, it will bleach your insides (if not worse), because that would make it hydrogen peroxide and not water. Naming and actual reality have a direct connection in physics, even as they do in morality and in metaphysics.

So the question arises, Why do we readily accept the restrictive absolutes of chemical structures but refuse to carry these absolutes into our moral framework? The answer is obvious: we simply do not want anyone else to dictate our moral sensitivities; we wish to define them ourselves. This is at the heart of our rejecting of God's first injunction. It has very little to do with the tree and everything to do with the seed of our rebellion, namely, autonomy. We wish to be a law unto ourselves.

Of course, we also wish to have control over the tree of life. We desire perpetual and autonomous existence—in effect, wanting to play God. Even though we did not author creation, we wish to author morality and take the reins of life. Combine the two attitudes, and it boils down to this: we want to live forever on our own terms.

In the first chapter of this book, I referred to the address I delivered at a prestigious university on the subject "What Does It Mean to Be Human?" A professor of medical ethics from another university had the next presentation. It didn't take long to sense that we were poles apart in our starting point. After listening to her views (neither medical nor ethical, it seemed to me, but rather just moral autonomy masquerading as science), she paid me the ultimate compliment. She said, "I have never met anybody with whom I have disagreed more." So I chose to agree with her on that point.

During the question and answer time that followed, a few things emerged. The first was her confident but naive optimism that, with all the tools in our hands, we could shape our future in genetics and engineer whatever we want to. She spoke in very altruistic terms about everything from the elimination of disease to the utilization of human cloning. Her arrogance, pathetic in its ignorance, added insult to injury when she gave not one whit of objective basis for what her ethical standards would be with regard to all of this.

When the organizers opened the floor to questions, one woman stood and said to me, "I was very offended by your comment that the heart of humanity is evil." Between the professor, who placed the power to live or die in human hands, and the questioner, who denied the depravity of the human heart, we had the garden of Eden in front of our eyes all over again. In Adam and Eve's defense, they, at least, felt ashamed after they had made the wrong choice. By contrast, our brilliant contemporaries have a chest-out, clenched-fist audacity and think that by shouting louder their arguments become truer.

I recall that Malcolm Muggeridge once said that human depravity is at once the most empirically verifiable fact yet most staunchly resisted datum by our intellectuals. For them, H_2O as the formula for water is indisputable; but in ethics, man is still the measure—without stating which man. This is the fundamental difference between a transcendent worldview and a humanistic one.

But the question arises as to what makes the Christian framework unique. Here we see the second cardinal difference between the Judeo-Christian worldview and the others. It is simply this: no amount of moral capacity can get us back into a right relationship with God.

The Christian faith, simply stated, reminds us that our fundamental problem is not moral; rather, our fundamental problem is spiritual. *It is not just that we are immoral, but that a moral life alone cannot bridge what separates us from God.* Herein lies the cardinal difference between the moralizing religions and Jesus' offer to us. Jesus does not offer to make bad people good but to make dead people alive.

Worldviews Apart

A brief glance at the basis of the laws that have come down to us through religious history gives us a clue. The Code of Hammurabi, originating in Eastern Mesopotamia, is one of the oldest legal codes we have, dating back to about 2500 BC. In addition to the preamble and the epilogue, it contains 282 prescriptions for conduct dealing with a wide range of situations. The last of the codes reads as follows: "If a slave say to his master, 'I am not your slave,' if they convict him, his master shall cut off his ear."

About a thousand years after this came the *Laws of Manu*, considered an arm of Vedic teaching. This codebook begins by telling us how ten sages went to the teacher Manu and asked him what laws should govern the four castes. The response came in 2,684 verses covering several chapters.

A few centuries later emerged the teachings of the Buddha, who rejected the caste system and built his prescription for conduct on "the four noble truths":

1. the fact of suffering;
2. the cause of suffering;
3. the cessation of suffering; and
4. the eightfold path that can end suffering

About a millennium later came Muhammad in the sixth century after Christ. His instructions came in the "five pillars [or injunctions]" of Islam: the Creed; the Prayers; the Tithe; the Fast; and the Pilgrimage (some add Jihad as the sixth). All of these are prescribed in specific ways. The injunctions address every detail imaginable. The Hadith (a narrative record of the sayings and traditions of Muhammad) became the basis of the practices and customs of all Muslims.

Approximately fourteen centuries before Christ (scholars debate the exact date), the Hebrew people received the Ten Commandments. An extraordinary first line gives the basis of the Ten Laws: "I am the LORD your God, who brought you out of Egypt, out of the land of slavery. You shall have no other gods before me" (Exodus 20:2–3).

To miss this preamble is to miss the entire content of the Mosaic law. It provides the clue to each of the systems of law that have emerged through time. Here the Hebrew-Christian worldview stands distinct and definitively different. *Redemption precedes morality, and not the other way around.* While every moral law ever given to humanity provides a set of rules to abide by in order to avoid punishment or some other retribution, the moral law in the Bible hangs on the redemption of humanity provided by God.

Something else emerges with stark difference. If you notice, the moral law in the other legal codes *separates* people (the Laws of Manu, the caste system, the Code of Hammurabi with the slave/owner distinction). In Islam, the violator is inferior to the obedient one. By contrast, in the Hebrew-Christian tradition, the law *unifies* people. No one is made righteous before God by keeping the law. It is only following redemption that we can truly understand the moral law for what it is—a mirror that indicts and calls the heart to seek God's help. This makes moral reasoning the fruit of spiritual understanding and not the cause of it.

The first four of the Ten Commandments have to do with our worship of God, while the next six deal with our resulting responsibilities to our fellow human beings. These commandments base a moral imperative on our spiritual commitment, first toward God and second toward humanity. This logic is unbreakable. We see the various components come into place—the exclusivity and supremacy of one God; the sacredness of his very name; the entanglement of means as they become ends in themselves; the sanctity of time as God gives it to us.

Taken in a single dimension, the Ten Commandments show us the transcending reality of God's existence and his distance from us. We cannot truly live without understanding this distance and who God is. Within this framework we learn that God blesses and judges, that his judgments can last generations from the deed, that his love deserves our ultimate pursuit, that worship is both timely and timeless. The human condition in and of itself cannot touch this reality. Any life that does not see its need for redemption will not understand the truth about morality.

A Universe Framed

When you look at the first book of the Bible, you begin to see very quickly what God meant when he pronounced his creation "good." God intended to create something good so that his creation would display his very *creative power* and his *communion goal*. Those twin realities framed the universe.

Human beings are born creators. They fashion their tools, discover new ways of doing things, find shortcuts, and revel in their new inventions. This genius reflects the very character of God and the capacity imbued by him to humanity. But here one also comes up against a serious challenge. Do boundaries have to be drawn, and do man's goals have to fit within those boundaries?

Recently, while sitting in the departure area of an airport, I read an advertisement that boasted, "No boundaries: Just possibilities." A tantalizing thought indeed. Are there really no boundaries to anything? If no boundaries exist for me, does it follow that no boundaries exist for everyone else? The most fascinating thing about the created order is that God set but one stipulation for humanity. Once humanity violated that single rule and took charge, however, *hundreds* of laws had to be passed, because each injunction could die the death of a thousand qualifications through constant exceptions to the rule.

The bane of my life is flying. I have to get on a plane at least two or three times a week. The wordiness of what we are not allowed to do while on board always intrigues me. The passenger hears that to tamper with, disable, or destroy the smoke detector in the bathroom of an airplane is a criminal offense. But could someone really destroy or disable it without tampering with it? The answer is yes, if it could be done without touching the device. But then again, the whole idea of tampering with the smoke detector really deals with its effectiveness in detecting smoke, doesn't it? Ah, but that's where we get into technicalities in a court of law. This manipulation of wording and morality lies at the core of all autonomy. The moral law will always stand over and above and against a heart that seeks to be its own guide.

One of my colleagues in ministry recently told me of a visit he had made to a mutual friend in Cape Town, South Africa. As they were enjoying the evening together, they heard a huge crash. It took them a few moments to locate its source, and when they went outside, they saw in the front of their driveway a car that had been literally smashed off its undercarriage. Someone hurtling along at a high rate of speed had missed a turn and had run headlong into the parked car. The driver, however, had managed to speed off.

My friends noticed a huge puddle of water at the scene and deduced that the fleeing culprit must have damaged his radiator and could not have gone far. So they jumped into their car and drove a hundred yards to a street corner. As they rounded the corner, they saw a steaming vehicle on the side of the road, with two teenagers standing alongside, looking shaken and bewildered and at a loss for what to do. It turned out that they had taken their dad's brand-new, high-priced vehicle without his knowledge. My friend Peter, a very successful businessman, as well as a very tenderhearted follower of Jesus Christ, pulled over next to the young men. Seeing them so shaken, Peter said, "May I pray with you and ask God to comfort you and see you through this ordeal?" The young men looked rather surprised but nodded their heads. Peter put his hands on their shoulders and prayed for them. No sooner had Peter said his "Amen" than one of the young fellows said, "If God loves me, why did he let this happen to me?"

Imagine the series of duplicitous acts that preceded that question, and you see the human heart for what it is. Did God set this boy up, or did the boy set God up? You see, when you understand that God determines the moral framework and that any violation of it is to usurp God, you learn that it is not God who has stacked the deck; the issue is our own desire to take God's place.

What Place, Then, for Morality?

While at a conference in another country, I was approached by a young woman, who asked if she could talk to me privately. Once we found a couple of chairs and sat down to talk, I learned that she was miles away from the land of her birth and had lived through some horrendous experiences. She had a beautiful mother, but her father, as she worded it, did not have the same admirable looks. Through an arranged marriage, they had begun their lives together, but the father always resented his wife's looks and the many compliments given to her, while none ever came his way. His distorted thinking took him beyond jealousy to fears that some man might lure her away, and so he made his plan to snuff out any such possibility. One day, he returned home, and while talking to his wife in their bedroom, he reached into his bag, grabbed a bottle of acid, and flung the contents into her face. In one instant, he turned his wife's face from beautiful to horrendously scarred. He then turned and fled from the house.

At the point of our conversation, two decades had gone by since mother and daughter had last seen him. The young woman, now in her twenties, had been a little girl when this tragic event took place, and yet the bitterness in her heart remained as fresh as the day she saw her mother's face turned from beauty to ugliness—so hideous that it forced the little one to cover her own face so she wouldn't have to see what had been done.

But the story did not end there. Just a few days before our conversation, the mother, who had raised the family on her own, had heard from the husband who had deserted her. He was dying of cancer and living alone. He wondered if she would take him back and care for him in this last stage of his illness. The audacious plea outraged this young woman. But the mother, a devout follower of Jesus Christ, pleaded with her children to let her take him back and care for him as he prepared to die.

In this story, we see all the elements of the human fall and the power of a redeemed heart. Morality alone would dictate that he gets what he deserves. A redeemed heart says, "Let me bind his wounds because what needs attention is his soul." Morality alone says, "There is nothing reasonable in the man's request." The redeemed heart says, "The reason by which we live is the heart of mercy that does not keep a ledger." Morality says, "It's all about whether you think it's right or not." The redeemed heart says, "What would God have me do in this situation?" Morality says, "Make your own judgments." The redeemed heart says, "Don't make a judgment unless you are willing to be judged by the same standard." In short, morality is a double-edged sword. It cuts the very one who wields it, even as it seeks to mangle the other.

I have often wondered if many who name the name of Jesus have missed this truth. I think, too, that in missing this, we miss the larger point often hidden in what appears to be the main point. When we stand before God, it would not surprise me to find out that the real point of the story of the prodigal son was really the older brother; that the real point of the good Samaritan was the priest and the Levite who went on their way; that the real point of the women arriving first at the tomb was that the disciples hadn't; that the real point of the story of Job was the moralizing friends. Those who play by the rules sometimes think that this is all there is to it and that they merit their due reward. Yet God repeatedly points out that without the redemption of the heart, all moralizing is hollow.

In the garden it was not we who were set up but we who tried to set God up by blaming him for the situation and then wishing to redefine everything. Had we obeyed everything, we still would have lost if we had errantly concluded that we deserved what the garden offered. What, then, of the moral law in the believer?

How does this work out in my own life? What place does the moral law have? The threads are many, the pattern complex — but the analysis is simple. Your moral framework is critical in the respect you show for yourself and your fellow human beings. Think of it as the coinage of your life and your day-to-day living. But this coinage has no value if it is not based on the riches of God's plan for your spiritual well-being.

Morality is the fruit of your knowledge of God, conscious or otherwise. But it can never be the *root* of your claim before God. Morality can build pride as well as philanthropy; true spirituality will never submit to pride. Having said all that, morality is still the ground from within which the creative spirit of art and other disciplines may grow. But if they grow to exaggerate who we are, then it is morality for morality's sake. If it sprouts toward heaven, it points others to God.

The moral law also serves as a profound reminder that in God there is no contradiction. The moral law stands as a consistent, contradiction-free expression of God's character. If I violate this law, I bring contradiction into my own life, and my life begins to fall apart. This is why a humble spirit, as it honors God, realizes how near and yet how far it is from God.

Point Others to the Source

C. S. Lewis has a remarkable little illustration in his book *The Screwtape Letters*. The senior devil is coaching the younger one on how to seduce a person who hangs between belief and disbelief in the Enemy (the Enemy here being God). So the younger one sets to work on keeping this man from turning to God. But in the end, after all the tricks and seductions, the individual is "lost to the Enemy." When the defeated junior devil returns, the senior one laments and asks, "How did this happen? How did you let this one get away?"

"I don't know," says the young imp. "But every morning he used to take a long walk, just to be quiet and reflective. And then, every evening he would read a good book. Somehow during those books and walks, the Enemy must have gotten his voice through to him."

"That's where you made your mistake," says the veteran. "You should have allowed him to take that walk purely for physical exercise. You should have had him read that book just so he could quote it to others. In allowing him to enjoy pure pleasures, you put him within the Enemy's reach."[5]

Lewis's brilliant insight applies to morality as well. Pure morality points you to the purest one of all. When impure, it points you to yourself. The purer your habits, the closer to God you will come. Moralizing from impure motives takes you away from God.

Let all goodness draw you nearer, and let all goodness flow from you to point others to the source of all goodness. God's conditions in the garden of Eden were not a setup, any more than the temptation of Jesus in the wilderness was a setup or that the long journey to Egypt was a setup. God wants us to understand our own hearts, and nothing shows this more than the stringent demands of a law that discloses we are not God—and neither had we better play God. Once we understand this and turn to him, we find out the truth of what the psalmist wrote: "To all perfection I see a limit, but [the Lord's] commands are boundless" (Psalm 119:96). True fulfillment and the possibility of boundless enjoyment come when we do life God's way. When we do it our way, we only enslave ourselves.

Some time ago, I was speaking at the University of South Queensland in Australia. It was shortly after the death of one of Australia's great entertainers, Steve Irwin. I was answering the question of whether there is meaning in suffering and evil from the Christian worldview; flanking me were a Muslim scholar and the local president of the Humanist Association. A question came from the floor about Steve Irwin's destiny. What did these worldviews have to say about this?

The humanist's answer was hollow, ignoring the issue of what happened after death: "Nothing really, just to celebrate a life now gone." That was it.

The Muslim said that Steve's good deeds would be measured against his bad deeds. That was it—a balance in hand with weights. It really was a clever answer that dodged the real question. So I asked him, "Are you saying that all of his good deeds would usher him to paradise?" He was quite taken aback by my question and stated that I was introducing a different issue. And so it is in his faith. In response, I noted that, based on the teachings of Jesus, morality was never a means of salvation for anyone. The moral threads of a life were intended to reflect and honor the God we served; they are not a means of entering heaven.

Why does a man honor his vows? Why does a woman honor her vows? Is it to earn the love of their spouse, or is it to demonstrate the sacredness of their love? True love engenders a life that honors its commitment. That is the role of obedience to God's moral precepts—putting hands and feet to belief, embodying the nature of what one's ultimate commitment reflects—the very character of God. Jesus said to let our lives so shine before people that they would glorify God as a result (see Matthew 5:16)—this is the end result of a life that takes the moral commands seriously.

So how does one pull together the strings in this whole business of morals? Whatever you do, whether it be at work or in marriage, through your language or your ambitions, in your thoughts or your intents, do all and think all to the glory of God (see 1 Corinthians 10:31) and by the rules he has put in place—rules that serve not to restrain us but to be the means for us to soar with the purpose for which he has designed all choices.

CHAPTER 5

Your Spirituality Matters

I WAS IN A HOTEL ROOM, PREPARING TO GIVE A SERIES OF LECTURES later that day. As the maid tidied up the room, she asked what had brought me to California. I told her I was speaking at the local university on the subject of God's existence. She continued fluffing up the pillows and said, "How exciting! I'm into metaphysics myself!" Surprised, I asked if she was a student at the university. "Oh, no," she said, "I just dabble in a lot of esoteric stuff."

"Metaphysics." "Esoteric." This new vocabulary allows one to discuss ultimate questions without having to offend anyone or defend anything. Something just has to be stated in order to be valid. This is the language of the new spirituality. It used to be said, "It can't be wrong when it feels so right." Now it may be said, "If you believe it, it has to be right."

Changes in language often reflect the changing values of a culture. Whether something is politically correct or culturally unacceptable depends on who is in political control and which culture enjoys favored status with the media.

As I was growing up in India, I read a story about a man who had two idols in his home. One was large and rather fierce looking. The other was small, with a cheery face. Every day, morning and night, the man would carry out his worship rituals—placing fruit offerings before the idols and chanting hymns, while his son watched with great curiosity. Finally his son said, "Why are you talking to stones? These are lifeless things. They can't speak or move or do anything, yet you spend all this time every day doing what you do."

The father grew very angry and reprimanded his son. "Don't you dare speak that way! These are not just stones! These are our gods! We worship them, and they protect us." The son realized he had touched a raw nerve and wisely decided to push the issue no further.

But one day, in the father's absence, the son took a big stick and smashed the little idol to pieces. Then he took the stick and placed it in the hands of the big idol. When evening came, his father walked into the house and, stunned by the sight, let out a shout. "Who did this? What happened here?"

The son came running into the room, pretending to be dismayed, and said, "It has to be the big one! Look, he has a stick in his hands!"

The suggestion infuriated the father, and he yelled, "Of course he couldn't have done it!"

"Why not?" asked his son.

"Because he's made of stone, that's why! He can't move! There's no life in him!"

The son dropped his act and said, "That's what I've been trying to tell you, haven't I?"

This obviously imaginary story makes a point. But are the gods we worship any less imaginary? Across time and across cultures, all kinds of beliefs have come and gone. One wonders how people believe some of the things they do. Sadly, some people may feel offended by my use of this story, believing that it disparages someone else's belief.

The Quest for the Spiritual

The emerging reality is twofold. First, we human beings are incurably religious. We long to worship and will even create our own objects of worship. All someone has to do to prove this is to take a trek around the globe.

Even as I write this chapter, the sound of chants reaches my ears. If I look out my window, I can see worshipers dancing as they burn incense to idols. Ironically, the founder of this particular religion did not even believe in any supernatural entity or power. Yet over the centuries his followers have become obsessed by superstition and simply cannot imagine living without their daily rituals.

Second, it is imperative that we know whether the object we worship truly deserves our worship and actually has the characteristics we ascribe to it. Does the God of the Qur'an really exist? Is the text of the Qur'an really inspired? Are the Hindu scriptures truly a revelation of the one ultimate reality? Are reincarnation and the caste system truly facts of life, or just beliefs passed on within a culture? Is the Christian faith true, and is Jesus who he claimed to be?

When Paul visited Athens, he saw numerous altars to various gods. In fact, the people had even set up an extra altar, just in case they had missed some deity and offended it (see Acts 17:16, 23). This is precisely the nature of spirituality today.

Why does Hinduism have three hundred and thirty million gods in its pantheon? Why has Buddhism, which is intrinsically atheistic, spawned such animistic and ritualistic codes of belief that the average believer cannot comprehend the philosophical ideas that shape his or her beliefs? Why is Christendom so plagued with "new" ideas and schemes that have duped the masses for centuries? In some incense-filled churches you can see the teeth of a revered saint and the tongue of another saint preserved in solution—and sadly, people kneeling before it and kissing the glass that separates them from these venerated objects. How has Islam persuaded millions that the only way to pray is to turn in the direction of Mecca and that you have to do it five times a day? (The original revelation to Muhammad called for prayer fifty times a day, but he interceded and got it reduced to five.) Evangelical Christianity is not immune to this tendency either. Every generation produces some new voice that promises to change the way we think, preaching a prosperity largely unavailable to the average person in the pew (except in dreams) but abundantly enjoyed by the preacher.

Our age-old quest for the spiritual is incurable. We always hope that something new will do what something old didn't. The skeptics are partly right that religion can be born out of fear and superstition. How do we counter the charge, and how do we rescue ourselves from pursuing spirituality for spirituality's sake?

Spirituality Dressed in Various Attire

Jesus challenged three different types of spirituality: traditionalism, legalism, and superstition. Each type has its own particular attraction and error.

Traditionalism

The traditionalist paid homage to the sects and groups that built their traditions around sayings and laws. Whether representing the Pharisees or the Sadducees, they had their own set of codes for conduct and belief—but managed only to weigh people down. I grew up in a culture like this. Some of these expectations can be serious, and some are almost comical; yet even so they inspire the same tenacity.

Some time ago, some of my friends and I visited the famed Kali temple in Calcutta, India. In the Hindu belief system,

Kali, the goddess of destruction, is one of the consorts of Lord Shiva. She has different names, but the common idea is that she can wreak havoc in a life that has grown out of tune with its spiritual roots. The Kali temple is also one of just two temples in India that still practices animal sacrifice. Watching the ritual leaves lasting memories.

The floor around the altar—blood-splattered and filthy—says it all. The family bringing the sacrifice pulls the rope tied around the neck of a little goat. The goat bleats and struggles, terribly nervous in the midst of all the commotion. A crowd gathers around the square. Inside, close to the altar, the family waits. The priest finally enters the square, a loincloth wrapped around his waist. He looks sweaty and preoccupied. Someone brings him the goat. He picks it up and places its head on a board between two vertical bars. Then, faster than the eye can see, the blade descends on its neck. In one swift motion, the priest grabs the beheaded carcass, still in spasms, and sets it aside.

On this occasion, as we watched in wonder, the priest took the carcass and flung it aside—and then swiveled toward us in anger before the carcass had even hit the ground. He yelled curses at the video cameraman who had photographed the procedure, in clear violation of the rules and the sacrifice's spiritual significance. A shoving match instantly ensued as he tried to grab the camera and break it. From chants and spiritual power to sudden rage—a short step in direction but a huge gap in sanctity. To him, the violation of the rules nullified the sacrifice. I sympathized with his reason for getting angry, but it seemed unreasonable that the gods should be impotent to act on the sacrifice because of a video camera.

The first time I saw this ritual sacrifice carried out, I remember so clearly the supplicant bending down and symbolically placing his head between the vertical bars. Then he put his fingers in the fresh blood of the goat, which had collected in a basin, and marked his spotless white shirt with it. The bloodstained shirt was his mark of identification. I recall asking a Hindu philosopher next to me why the man carried out this symbolic act. He shook his head and said, "Nothing. It means nothing."

But in this instance, even as the man touched the blood to his shirt, the priest vented his outrage at the offending cameraman with an intensity and fury that had everyone scampering as fast as they could in the opposite direction. If, as the Hindu philosopher had told me, the sacrifice meant "nothing," then why did the priest react with such rage? The truth is that it is not "nothing."

Over the centuries, spiritual ceremony quickly becomes more important than what it facilitates. We cannot help but wonder why intelligent people do not seem to question its basis in truth. Jesus consistently raised concerns about rote sacrifice and ceremony. In the Old Testament, the prophets express the same concerns. The prophet Micah declared these memorable words:

> With what shall I come before the LORD
>   and bow down before the exalted God?
> Shall I come before him with burnt offerings,
>   with calves a year old?
> Will the LORD be pleased with thousands of rams,
>   with ten thousand rivers of oil?
> Shall I offer my firstborn for my transgression,
>   the fruit of my body for the sin of my soul?

MICAH 6:6–7

The people to whom Micah spoke had practiced every activity mentioned in the passage. The search for spirituality, or its expression, will not stop, even at offering its own offspring to somehow ease a guilty conscience. The apostle Paul goes so far as to say that Satan deceives and even controls lives through expressions rooted in belief and shrouded in ceremony (see Romans 1:21–25). As daunting and discomforting a thought as this is, the Scriptures clearly warn us that a lie that begins as comfortable all too often proceeds to self-deification and ultimately to self-deception and self-destruction. In the warning brought by the prophet Habakkuk, we hear God asking, "Of what value is an idol, since a man has carved it? Or an image that teaches lies?" (2:18). The prophet goes on to remind the people that in this process they have, in effect, become the "creators," worshiping their own "creation."

Probably the most terrifying passage that shows how such ceremony leads to self-destruction is 2 Kings 21:1–6, where we read that the ceremonies and altars established by Manasseh in his efforts to create his own spirituality finally resulted in the sacrificing of his own son to the burning arms of the idol. Few delusions are more error prone than a form of spirituality that hides the hollowness of substance. The enemy of our souls can use ceremony and ritual based on falsehood to control us and enslave us to error.

Legalism

Jesus also challenged the spirituality of legalism—strict conformity to a religious or moral code. Somehow we think that if we keep the law meticulously, we will be safe from God's wrath. Consider the following example.

During a visit I made to an Islamic country, I befriended a taxi driver, a man in his fifties, who drove me around the city for several days. He talked freely about his life and his rituals. He told me that he had two wives—only because he couldn't afford more. One wife was about his age, and the second one was in her twenties. He talked—sometimes crudely—about which wife served which purpose. Then he talked about the immorality and the duplicity of the West and railed on the West out of the context of his own political views.

One day I asked him if he had yet gone on the pilgrimage to Mecca.

"Oh, no! Oh, no! That will not be for me for some time."

"Why not?" I asked.

He eased up on the gas pedal, tapped the meter that was not running, and said, "Do you know why this is installed? To deny me the living that I can make without it. If I charged you what I am allowed to by law, I couldn't feed my family. I have to cheat customers in order to survive. And if I make the pilgrimage, I will not be able to cheat them. Once the *Hajj* is taken, I will be bound by religious obligations that I cannot keep." He would not take the pilgrimage because he wanted no entailments from that journey. But that was not all.

"You have just raised a very interesting question in my mind," I said. "You told me some time ago that you did not trust many politicians. Yet many of them added the title *hajji* to their name that shows they have taken the *Hajj*, perhaps many times. How is it that you do not trust someone who has evidently made the pilgrimage?"

"Oh, sir!" he replied. "You are an Easterner, and you ask such questions? You know that our politicians are corrupt. They use religion for power, but they do not follow that religion and its real values."

That said it all—the mix of ritual, power, spirituality, and obligation. This man did not recognize the same self-defeating posture in his own life that he saw in the politicians. To him, religion meant a plethora of rules and expectations, out of which he then decided which ones to abide by and which ones not to abide by. But when the politician did the same, he or she was corrupt. This taxi driver illustrates how religion functions for millions of people in our world.

Jesus encountered repeatedly those who "lived by the law" and used the law to condemn others, yet who never saw the spirit behind the law. Legalistic thinking is another of those "spiritual expressions."

Superstition

The third type of spirituality, namely, superstition, controls millions of people. I remember being in a Hindu home and meeting the family for the first time. It was a Thursday. One member of the family warned me that I would be offered no food or drink because it was the first time I was coming into their home, and to offer food or drink to a first-time guest arriving on a Thursday would be a bad omen. So despite the hospitable culture, they could offer me nothing because of a fondly held superstition. I got some lunch outside the home, but I could not eat it inside, as that could have spelled disaster. I told the family member that I might someday write a book called *Superstitions and Their Origins*. She smiled and said, "It wouldn't change my mom's belief any."

This is a huge trap. My own mother woke up every morning, reached for her glasses, and looked at the picture of Jesus and the picture of Saint Philomena hanging next to it before she cast her eyes on anything else. My mother revered Saint Philomena because she felt sure it was the prayers of the saint to whom she had interceded that kept my sister from dying of polio when she was only five days old. My mother insisted on looking at the saint's picture before each day began.

Jesus spoke a great deal about the superstitions that snared the masses of his time. In Mark 7, Jesus reserves his strongest words for those for whom appearance, tradition, and ceremony have become the supreme demonstration or mark of spirituality. He compares them to a cup that looks clean on the outside but is actually unwashed within, and to whitewashed tombs that look beautiful on the outside but are filled with death and decay on the inside (see Matthew 23:25–27). Of such people,

Jesus says, "These people honor me with their lips, but their hearts are far from me. They worship me in vain; their teachings are but rules taught by men" (Matthew 15:8–9).

Jesus would not have used such strong language if this issue of false spirituality initiated by humanity in our own efforts at religion were not of such a serious nature. Superstition and ritual may have innocent beginnings, like wading into what one thinks is a shallow pool, but its undercurrent will paralyze true worship.

The Modern-day Spiritualist

I find it fascinating to observe how variations of all these spiritualities have appeared in our day and how it has become worthy of a medal of honor to say, "I believe in spirituality." But what does such a phrase mean? I believe that the speaker is really saying, "I believe that there is such a thing as the spiritual beyond the physical—some combination of the mystical and the ethical. I believe that everyone must find something spiritual to hang on to in life. I believe that life is not just physical."

In the midst of these affirmations, however, two untruths get smuggled in. The first is that truth does not matter, only belief; and the second is that to be spiritual is to be Eastern. The stranger the sound of the term, the more useful it must be. Within the expressions of these two errors, we are seeing ideas that strain credulity.

Think of it as the "organic foods version" for the soul. "Karma," "Tantra," "chakra"—even "yoga"—have mutated into Western garb. Caught in a traffic jam recently in Atlanta, I saw a bumper sticker on the car in the lane beside me that read, "Jesus is my co-pilot." On the car directly in front of me, a bumper sticker read, "Chant om for peace."

Some years ago, I spoke at a conference in the Philippines. One evening when I returned to my hotel, the manager asked if I could take a few minutes to visit with an Australian couple staying in a room with their twelve-year-old son. The manager was an interesting woman with a master's degree in philosophy. She and I had enjoyed a few interesting discussions at night when I had returned from the meetings. When I asked why she wanted me to visit them, she said that their son was dying of cancer. She felt this couple needed some "spiritual" help and thought I might want to pray with them. When I knocked on their door, they were expecting me.

They had a sad story to tell. Their little boy was in the final stages of cancer. They had heard about a faith healer in the Philippines who claimed to be able to "dig" into the human body and extract the tumor without making an incision, and so they had traveled from Australia with their emaciated son to present him to this man. There the boy lay, in a room smelling of stale air and medication. Already he looked almost like a corpse, not moving or making any sound.

"Have you seen this man who is to heal him?" I asked.

"Yes, indeed. See this jar on the table? It contains the tumor he scraped out of our boy's body, roots and all. We got it. He was brilliant. It's just amazing!"

I stood there quietly, taking in all the signs of looming death in the room. I listened with great sadness to this refrain of optimism that seemed to say that if they repeated the hope often enough, it would become reality. I couldn't hold back the tears. These good people had been had—big-time. Their vulnerability and their longing had sent them into the clutches of a charlatan. Their son was visibly close to death. It seemed as though the only thing left to do was to pull the sheet over the boy's fragile body. Yet they clung to this faith healer's magic.

I sat down and lingered with them awhile. I just let them talk. They had scheduled a flight back to Australia for early the next morning. Were they leaving quickly in order to avoid facing the community in the event that they had been duped? I didn't know. I prayed for them, that God would be with them through this difficult time and sustain them in their need. When I left their room, I gave them my business card and said, "When you return home, if your son really starts to pull through, will you please drop me a note so that I can know that this was for real?" They assured me they would, but I never heard from them again. The manager told me that thousands of people come to the Philippines for that very reason—to visit faith healers—and then leave, fooled by these masters of "sleight of hand."

Spiritual seduction is the deadliest of all seductions because it barters away the soul. Just look at the cults around us. Some deny any physical reality; others tell us that we came from extraterrestrial aliens; still others come to our doors and predict the end of the world. The threads of spirituality run through all of our lives.

The Ultimate Spirituality

How does one find the right threads to bring about the perfect design? By far, the most important thread is *truth*—and yet the death of truth has been the single greatest casualty of our time.

In no segment of society can we survive without truth. Whether the setting is in the courts or in the marriage bond, we simply cannot live without truth. Truth will sooner or later catch up to us, and we will have to pay its dues.

When we observe the history of thought, we see humanity swinging from one extreme to the other. The terminology is big—rationalism, empiricism, existentialism, postmodernism. In each of these ways of looking at reality, unfortunately, one thread dominated and obliterated the others. In rationalism it was reason above all else. In empiricism it was scientific single-vision. In existentialism it was the triumph of the will in the face of despair. In postmodernism it was the absence of absolute truth as something that is possible to know. God remarkably gives each one its rightful place.

The scientist must test his or her theories by observation and verification—but how does one find out whether someone ought to honor his or her marital vows? To do this requires a worldview, and that worldview must be subjected to the tests of truth.

In 1995, the famed football player O.J. Simpson went on trial for the murders of his wife, Nicole Brown Simpson, and Nicole's friend Ronald Goldman. The whole episode captivated the nation's attention. I remember trying to buy something in a store and not being able to find anyone to help me—all the salesclerks had planted themselves in front of the television set, absorbed in the trial. Robert Shapiro first represented Mr. Simpson, followed by Johnny Cochrane. Clearly, a very strong individual had committed the brutal killing. Prosecutors had accumulated some powerful evidence. Everything pointed to Simpson as the murderer, from physical evidence to his subsequent behavior. But cleverly worded arguments, the famed glove the prosecution made him try on (a glove that had shrunk due to dried-up blood), and accusations of racial motivations all added fuel to the fire, and in the end, the jury acquitted him.

After the verdict, I found the interviews given by the attorneys to be most interesting. When Larry King asked Robert Shapiro on live television, "What do you think is the truth about that night, Bob?" Shapiro answered cavalierly, "It's not our job to deal with the truth, Larry." One wonders if Mr. Shapiro would have felt the same emotional distance from the truth had his daughter been the murder victim. (Johnny Cochrane, now sadly deceased from brain cancer, has certainly discovered that truth does matter.) Most fascinating of all, perhaps, is that no one is looking for the murderer, including Mr. Simpson, even though after his acquittal he vowed he would never give up the search for the "real killer." Months later, one journalist quipped that one may conclude that Nicole Brown Simpson's killer must be on a golf course, judging by the amount of time Simpson was spending there.

The tragedy is that when truth dies, people are sacrificed at the altar of pragmatism and manipulated by words in the human game of one-upmanship. God plays no such games. When Satan tempted Jesus in the desert, he didn't use new tricks. The temptation ultimately came down to doing the right thing for the wrong reason. Satan positioned one of his temptations with the words, "It is written," and Jesus ultimately dismissed Satan with a proposition of his own: "Away from me, Satan! For it is written ..."

Why did the devil quote Scripture, and why did Jesus respond with the larger context of Scripture? Words are bearers of thought, and reason must bear the responsibility of checking the text and the context. Truth is communicated principally through propositions. That is why the word is so important.

But this ploy of Satan is not really new, is it? Take a text out of context, and you make it a pretext. The context of life reminds us again and again that where you see intelligence in the result, you see a mind behind the result. But naturalists who are determined to do away with God debunk the notion of design with designed arguments. So they take a text out of context, betraying their own pretext to turn away from reason. The net result is a life detached from its moorings. Life simply cannot be lived that way, and so spirituality comes in through the back door, offering an escape from the barrenness of naturalism. But without truth, the threads do not make a beautiful design. Without truth, spirituality is nothing more than a confession that sheer matter alone does not answer life's deepest hungers.

How does one find the thread of truth? By looking at the One who claimed to be the Truth—Jesus Christ. In him, "the Word became flesh and made his dwelling among us ..., full of grace and truth" (John 1:14). Truth, with its handmaiden of grace, was incarnate in Jesus Christ. With Jesus in your life, the most important thread holds everything else together.

Jesus and Truth

In the gospel of Matthew, we receive a brilliant insight into Jesus' handling of a legalistic and ceremonial spirituality. Jesus had been walking through some fields of grain on a Sabbath day. According to Mosaic law, grain could not be picked on the Sabbath. But the hungry disciples reached out to pick some grain and began to eat it as they walked along. Naturally, the "spiritualists" jumped on that violation of the law and asked Jesus how he could condone such a thing. Jesus, as always, responded to hypocritical or unreflective questions with a question of his own:

> "Haven't you read what David did when he and his companions were hungry? He entered the house of God, and he and his companions ate the consecrated bread—which was not lawful for them to do, but only for the priests. Or haven't you read in the Law that on the Sabbath the priests in the temple desecrate the day and yet are innocent? I tell you that one greater than the temple is here. If you had known what these words mean, 'I desire mercy, not sacrifice,' you would not have condemned the innocent. For the Son of Man is Lord of the Sabbath."
>
> MATTHEW 12:3–8

Jesus took the law's severity and showed his hearers that, technically, both the people and the priests violate it all the time. He pointed out that the ceremony had a larger point than mere ritual, namely, that he was Lord of the Sabbath, which meant that all ceremonial law was designed to focus on him.

Yet over time, the ceremony became an end in itself and lost its true focus.

In Matthew 12, Jesus said three remarkable things in his response to the accusations that were being brought against him: he was greater than the temple (verse 6); he was greater than Jonah (verse 41); and he was greater than Solomon (verse 42). As greater than the temple, Jesus meant that he could be worshiped anywhere; he was the object of all the law and worship. That Jesus was greater than Solomon meant that Solomon's wisdom was mere theory and not practice; Jesus lived a life of perfection and true wisdom. That Jesus was greater than Jonah meant that Jonah had survived the catastrophe of spending three days inside a large fish—undoubtedly a miracle; Jesus would conquer death itself and three days after his death would rise again.

In effect, Jesus said that he is greater than religion, greater than any religious teacher, and greater than any miracle. True spirituality is not a religion, a "guru," or a miracle. True spirituality must follow where all these lead in ultimate truth—and that is to Jesus Christ alone.

The Most Important Question of All

Pilate asked the most important question of all time: "What is truth?" (John 18:38). Ironically, Pilate gloried in the question and never waited for the answer. Jesus had just said to him, "Everyone on the side of truth listens to me" (verse 37). One measures true spirituality by whether one listens to Jesus' voice. Asking Jesus the questions while refusing to listen to his answers reveals the ultimate hypocrisy and prejudice.

Elsewhere Jesus said, "The truth will set you free" (John 8:32). Did you know that two major universities in the United States (Southern Methodist University and Johns Hopkins University) use Jesus' words as their motto? But it seems they have failed to remember Jesus' preceding words: "If you hold to my teaching, you are really my disciples. Then you will know the truth, and the truth will set you free" (verses 31–32).

The most important question you will ever ask is, "What is truth?"—and on the heels of that, "Why does it matter?" Our society has struggled with these questions and has concluded that truth cannot be known, especially when it comes to ultimate matters. Jesus challenges this assumption. The word, the truth, Jesus' person, and true freedom are inextricably connected. This is the design God has made for you and for me. Break this design, and you break life. Honor this design, and you find true freedom.

Truth is the thread that separates true spirituality from false spirituality. Spirituality does not give relevance to life; rather, truth gives relevance to spirituality. You must not dare to get sidetracked with ceremony or legalism! Your spirituality must be born of the truth and lived out in grace.

Your spirituality matters to God, and it must matter to you as well.

CHAPTER 6

Your Will Matters

———◆·••·◆———

In September 1985, *Readers Digest* ran a story titled "Letter in the Wallet," written by Arnold Fine. Fine tells how one bitterly cold day he stumbled upon a wallet on the street. It had just three dollars in it and a crumpled-up letter that obviously had been carried around for many years. The letter was dated sixty years earlier and began, "Dear Michael." The beautifully written, sadly worded letter ended a romance because of a parent's demands. The last line promised, "I will always love you, Michael," and was signed, "Yours, Hannah."

Fine decided to try to track down the owner of the wallet. Using Hannah's address, still legible on the letter, he finally retrieved a telephone number. But when he called it, he was disappointed (though not surprised) to learn that Hannah and her family had long ago moved out of the house. The person on the other end of the line, however, knew the name of the nursing home to which Hannah's mother had gone. So Fine called the nursing home and learned that Hannah's mother was no longer living. When he told them what he was trying to do, however, they gave him the address and telephone number they had on file for Hannah. He called the number and found out that Hannah herself now lived in a nursing home. Fine asked for the name of the home and found the phone number. Soon he was able to confirm that, yes, Hannah was a resident there. As soon as he could, Fine decided to visit the nursing home and try to talk with Hannah.

The director met him at the door and told him that Hannah was watching television on the third floor. An escort quickly took Fine there and then left. Fine introduced himself to Hannah and explained how he had found a letter in a wallet. He showed her the letter and asked if she was the one who had written it.

"Yes," Hannah replied, "I sent this letter to Michael because I was only sixteen and my mother wouldn't let us see each other anymore. He was very handsome, you know, like Sean Connery." Fine could see both the twinkle in her eye and the joy on her face that spoke of her love for Michael. "Yes, Michael Goldstein was his name. If you find him, tell him that I think of him often and never did marry anyone. No one ever matched up to him," she declared, discreetly brushing tears from her eyes. Fine thanked her for her time and left.

As Mr. Fine was leaving the home, the security guard at the door asked him about his visit. He told the story and said, "At least I was able to get the last name from her. His name is Michael Goldstein."

"Goldstein?" repeated the guard. "There's a Mike Goldstein who lives here on the eighth floor." Fine turned around and went back inside, this time to the eighth floor, where he asked for Michael Goldstein. When directed to an elderly gentleman, he asked the man, "Have you lost your wallet?"

"Oh, yes, I lost it when I was out for a walk the other day," Michael answered.

Fine handed him the wallet and asked if it was his. Michael was delighted to see it again and, full of gratitude to the finder, proceeded to thank him for returning it when Fine interrupted him.

"I have something to tell you," Fine admitted. "I read the letter in your wallet."

Caught off guard, Michael paused for a moment and then asked, "You read the letter?"

"Yes, sir, and I have further news for you," Fine continued. "I think I know where Hannah is."

Michael grew pale. "You know where she is? How is she?"

"She's fine, and just as pretty as when you knew her."

"Could you tell me where she is? I'd love to call her. You know, when that letter came to me, my life ended. I've never gotten married. I never stopped loving her."

"Come with me," said Fine. He took Michael by the elbow and led him to the elevator and down to the third floor. By this time, the director of the building had rejoined them. They came to Hannah's room

"Hannah," the director whispered, gesturing toward Michael, "Do you know this man?"

She adjusted her glasses and looked at the man as she searched her memory bank. Then with a choked voice, Michael spoke up. "Hannah, it's Michael." She stood, as he walked over to her. They embraced and held on to each other for as long as they could stay steady on their feet. They sat down, holding hands, and between their tears they filled in the story of the long years that had passed. Feeling as though they had intruded on a sacred moment, Mr. Fine and the director slowly slipped away to leave the two alone to enjoy their reunion.

Three weeks later, Arnold Fine received an invitation to attend the wedding of Hannah, seventy-six years of age, and Michael, seventy-eight. Fine closes his story by saying, "How good the work of the Lord is."

Such a touching story can make one believe that it had to have been made in heaven. But think about it. Made in heaven it could be; the work of a sovereign God leaves all of us overwhelmed at the way God weaves the threads. At the same time, three determined wills all played a role here. A man loved his girl so much that he stayed faithful to her and remained single his whole life because he could not love another woman in this same way. A woman remained true to her first love, though she had been just a teenager, and she committed to honoring her parents' wishes. A man had resolved to return a wallet because he thought a poignant little letter kept for six decades merited a determined search for the owner.

The will is a strong but fragile part of every human life, and it matters in the rich weaving of your tapestry that is in the making.

The Exercise of Our Wills

This is both a theologically complex and an experientially difficult point to understand. Stories of the determination of those who persevere through bitter struggles thrill us, and our hearts feel disappointment when we read other stories that tell of the fickleness of those who flee at the slightest challenge. I will not venture here onto the mysterious terrain where God's sovereignty and human responsibility meet in the grand scheme of salvation. But I do want to focus on how we pursue our discipleship before God and on the threads in our tapestry that are pulled together by the exercise of our wills.

When God brings us to salvation, the most remarkable thing we see is that he transforms our hungers. He changes not just what we do but what we *want* to do. This is the work of the Holy Spirit within us—"for it is God who works in you to will and to act according to his good purpose" (Philippians 2:13). In our new walk, we make choices that help shape the design into something beautiful. These are the "wills" and the "won'ts."

Our society often fails to come to terms with this area of the will. Why do we shun it so? Mainly because it is difficult and persistent. Yesterday's victory does not guarantee tomorrow's. The relentlessness of the enemy of our souls demands that we remain ever watchful, and that's the hard part. We want results without effort. We want a lifestyle, but we don't really know what life is about. We want success without having to pay the price to get there. We want straight As, but we don't want to study. We want a blessed marriage, but we don't want the effort and commitment that it takes.

Certain keys to the will can unlock the huge potential God has placed within human power. Rightly understood, it yields humility; wrongly understood, it yields arrogance. Three scenes in the Bible put the will at the center of the discussion.

Writing Down Your Purpose

We find the first scene in Joshua's farewell address given to his people after they had crossed over the Jordan and came into contact with many seductive foreign gods. Joshua very plainly retraces for them all that God had done for generations in guarding them, delivering them in times of trouble, and keeping them in his care. He protected them in their forty years of wandering, during which time they learned many bitter lessons. Joshua had succeeded Moses, and now, as he was about to leave them to the care of others, he gave a very straightforward plea: "Choose for yourselves this day whom you will serve" (Joshua 24:15). No one could mistake that the choice of service to God lay in the will of the people. But this choice did not come in a vacuum. God presented it to them within the context of his work in their lives and his choice to bless them.

We must take hold of God's promise to bless us. He does not want us to struggle without his voice or his wisdom. He brings us to the place of his choosing, one way or the other. God could easily use a sledgehammer approach and "enforce" his will. He could make the Terminator look tame by comparison. But with infinite patience God works away in our lives, giving us sign after sign of his love — more often than not it goes unnoticed by most of us. Jesus asked the apostle Paul, "Why do you persecute me?" (Acts 9:4) and then went on to say to Paul, "It is hard for you to kick against the goads" (verse 5 NKJV). In effect, he was saying to Paul, "Why are you bloodying yourself against the markers God has placed along your way?"

Earlier I told the story of Ban Sanook, the "Fun House" in Chiang Mai, Thailand, established by a Japanese foundation to teach those who have disabilities how to weave silk (see page 26). As I walked into the home for the first time, all who sat at the weavers' bench wore casual dress. But two young people wore clothing a little more formal than the others. It was their duty that day to serve coffee and tea to the guests, hence the dressier attire. As they learn to serve, they also learn how to practice good personal hygiene, how to make a cup of coffee, how to make change for anyone who makes a purchase, and how to clean up the kitchen. It thrilled me to see how flattered they feel that they can wait on tables and take an order, then persist in the challenge to count and make change. The process also takes great patience on the part of the guest.

The man who birthed the vision for this place sat down with me one day and told me the story, both tragic and remarkable, of each child. He proceeded to tell me about the highlight of the week for them, when children from local elementary schools come to visit—children who perform tasks in the average to high range. He says, "It is a sight to see the young people with autism and Down syndrome teaching weaving and dancing to those not touched by any visible disability." He showed me pictures of the schoolchildren sitting at the looms and the "disabled ones" looking over their shoulders as the instructors. I asked, "Do they really teach?" He paused and said with a chuckle, "Teach and disturb at the same time."

But then with emotion in his eyes, he said, "When you think of how serious their debilitations are and yet how much laughter we hear here all the time, and when you see the finished works of art that fill this room, I get a little impatient when the not-so-afflicted in my circle of family or friends tell me they're not doing well because of a headache or a cold. I'm afraid I have become unsympathetic to our minor problems that we make so much of."

It made me think of how easily we take for granted the gift of being "normal." Sometimes those of us who have been blessed the most seem to be the least capable of seeing God's gracious hand on us. In our popular jargon, all catastrophes are "acts of God." By inference, our successes are "fate" or "good luck" or the results of sheer "individual effort." Legend has it that a corporal once said to Winston Churchill, "I want you to know, sir, that I am a self-made man." "Young man, you have just relieved God of a solemn responsibility," replied Churchill.

Like the old maestro who can make a melody out of the one remaining string on a broken instrument, God can show us the pattern of our lives if we will just see his gracious hand that has brought us this far already. We would do well, as Jacob did, to put up stone markers to remind us of God's goodness to us in specific situations: "I will build an altar to God, who answered me in the day of my distress and who has been with me wherever I have gone" (Genesis 35:3).

But this major step of making a choice to follow God entails one nonnegotiable commitment: to recognize the mission of your life not so much as a profession but as a measuring stick by which you will gauge your progress for life itself. Out of this emerges a commitment that your life express total submission to God's will. Reaching this point becomes most defining after you have spent time considering what it means, and then ideally have found a text of Scripture that encapsulates that pursuit. Such a thread is of incalculable worth.

Have you ever worked for a company that did not know why it existed? One of my favorite television commercials shows a group of men and women around a boardroom table in a serious and agitated discussion over some computer problems that have plagued the company. Finally one young man speaks up and says, "What about the shirts?"

"What about them?" demands the boss.

"Isn't that what this company is all about—manufacturing shirts?" comes the response.

The commercial suggests that too often we put all our energies into the peripheral concerns of life and forget why we are here. We neglect the purpose of our life.

The bane of our lives is getting sidetracked into secondary pursuits. Joshua reminds us that each of us must deliberately choose whom we will serve. So write down your purpose. Place it somewhere in a prominent spot so that you will continually be reminded of that purpose.

Cliff Barrows, Billy Graham's associate, told me that he always followed a particular practice when he checked into a hotel room. Before doing anything else, he put a picture of his family in a prominent place in the room. "It was a reminder to me and a signal to all who entered my room of my moral obligation to my family," he said. This is exactly what I mean. Mark down your life's goal, which will then provide you with the measuring stick you need to determine whether attractions and distractions are legitimate or illegitimate.

Susanna Wesley was a remarkable woman who gave birth to nineteen children. One can only guess the inner strength she must have had to raise John and Charles, two among many others who sat on her knee and learned from her to walk with the Lord. One day, John asked her to define sin. I doubt any theologian could have done better than she did: "Son, whatever weakens your reasoning, impairs the tenderness of your conscience, obscures your sense of God, or takes away your relish for spiritual things; in short, if anything increases the authority and power of the flesh over the Spirit, then that to you becomes sin, however good it is in itself."[1] That definition became the guiding beacon for John. He carved it into his consciousness. His mother inbred in him his sensitivity to sin.

I think of another example. As a young man, David Livingstone prayed, "Lord, send me anywhere, only go with me. Lay any burden on me, only sustain me. Sever any ties but the tie that binds me to your service and to your heart."[2] That prayer became his watchword when God laid Africa on his heart. I think of that remarkable line: "Sever any ties but the tie that binds me to your service and to your heart." What a mission statement for life! To be bound to God's service and to his heart! Set the purpose clearly before you.

Doing What's Right

The second scene occurs in Acts 22, where Paul recounts God's working in his life and the Lord's description of Paul's life mission. While Paul is recuperating from his blindness, Ananias says to him, "The God of our fathers has chosen you to know his will and to see the Righteous One and to hear words from his mouth" (Acts 22:14). Paul has a clearly distinctive encounter when he "sees and hears."

We also see this definite instruction to the apostle Thomas to see, touch, and hear the risen Lord. After Thomas obeys Jesus' instructions and recognizes him for who he really is, Jesus says to him, "Because you have seen me, you have believed; blessed are those who have not seen and yet have believed" (John 20:29). In the same chapter, when Mary saw the risen Jesus and literally wanted to hold on to him, Jesus said, "Do not hold on to me.... Go instead to my brothers and tell them" (verse 17). And again in the same chapter, as Jesus bids his disciples farewell, he says to them, "Receive the Holy Spirit" (verse 23).

In all of these instances, we note a presence, a voice, and a direction. We do not see, feel, and touch God. We do not, as a rule, hear his audible voice. Usually we hear God's voice to us through his written Word. That hearing must constantly be paired with "doing." It is amazing how many times we see in Scripture the word "do" combined with the term "the will of God." Jesus speaks of seeking not his own will but the will of the Father (see John 4:34; 6:38). "If anyone chooses to *do* God's will," Jesus says in John 7:17 (emphasis added). Revealing, knowing, and doing—these are the implicit ideas. In this context, we learn that God really does reveal his will; and if we walk in the known will of the Father, he reveals aspects of his will not so easily known. The hard part is to do that part of his will we already know.

How do we accomplish this, and how do we know for sure what God wants us to do in life's complex situations? This is where a battle rages within us over doing God's will. The apostle Paul said it best in Romans 7:15, 24: "For what I want to do I do not do, but what I hate I do.... What a wretched man I am! Who will rescue me from this body of death?" The seemingly endless struggle of willing and doing takes its toll. Often we cry out to God, "If only I knew the right choice here!"

Paul again gives us the clue in Romans 8:9: "You, however, are controlled not by the sinful nature but by the Spirit, if the Spirit of God lives in you." Here is the common ground to which all who approach God for power must come. Paul reminds us that the law lacks power (see Romans 8:3) because it was only a prescription, and no prescription by itself can bring rescue. Following the prescription does not solve the problem, for only the Holy Spirit has the power to rescue.

Unfortunately, so much theological fluff comes our way when we discuss the Holy Spirit, and so much misguided teaching has confused people about the Holy Spirit that we have forgotten the most important aspect of the Spirit's presence: the power that he gives us to do God's will. "Those who live according to the sinful nature have their minds set on what that nature desires; but those who live in accordance with the Spirit have their minds set on what the Spirit desires," writes Paul (Romans 8:5). But there are times when we throw up our hands and say, "But it's too hard! How can we do all that it takes to walk in obedience?" God speaks to that as well.

It Can Be Done

We witness the third scene in the book of Jeremiah (chapter 35). God asks the prophet to visit a small group of people called the Recabites, invite them to the temple, and in a side room offer them some wine to drink. Jeremiah makes the arrangements and brings them into the temple. After he seats them in the side room, he brings out a tray of glasses filled with wine, just as God had instructed him. But strangely, as he enters the room he becomes aware of discomfort among his guests.

"I'm sorry," says the leader of the group. "Didn't you know that we don't drink wine and that we haven't done so for generations? One of our ancestors, a very devout man, commanded us never to drink wine or to live in buildings. So to this day, we and our children and our grandchildren will never drink wine, and we live only in tents."

Jeremiah, surely mystified by the whole episode, must have wondered why God would give such instructions when he already knew that the Recabites did not drink wine. God explained, in effect, by telling Jeremiah, "I just wanted you to see a living example of how it is possible even for an earthly father to command such implicit obedience that it lasts for generations. But I have spoken to my people again and again, yet they have not obeyed me but have kept on making excuses for not serving me, their heavenly Father."

God makes a strong and compelling point. We are fully capable of exercising our wills to do what we have set our minds to do. Just observe those who follow earthly leaders.

This is where the hard questions of the Christian faith come to the fore. The gospel declares that the Holy Spirit brings about the new birth and that because of the Spirit's power within us, we gain the ability to do God's will. In other words, the new birth and the new walk are supernaturally bestowed. If by the sheer power of the will even a "pagan" is able to comply with a tough set of rules for living, then what does it say of the Christian who supposedly is supernaturally endowed but lives a duplicitous life? This is a hard question for the believer to answer. Only in and through the power of the Holy Spirit is the Christian walk even possible.

Submitting to God's Will

So where does one begin? With self-crucifixion. In effect, we go to our own funeral and bury the self-will so that God's will can reign supremely in our hearts. Our will has no power to do God's will until it first dies to its own desires and the Holy Spirit brings a fresh power within.

I well recall the first sermon I ever preached. I substituted for a young man who didn't show up for the engagement. I stood in front of the audience, completely terrified. Before I entered the tent where I was to speak, I fell on my knees, pleading with God to help me not to faint from fear. Once I stood up, it felt as though another power and another voice had taken hold of me.

The second time I preached, I had no doubt whatsoever of what was happening inside me. I knew that a power greater than myself was working out God's will and proclaiming his message. To this day I am absolutely convinced that when you work under God's will and your will submits to that will, you become a different person before people.

The ABCDs of a Willful Walk with the Lord

Out of these experiences, I developed what I call "the ABCDs of a willful walk with the Lord":

> **A**sk without pettiness
> **B**eing before doing
> **C**onvictions without compromise
> **D**iscipline without dreariness

Ask without Pettiness

The Bible tells us to *ask* for the Holy Spirit. In Luke 11 Jesus responds to a request from his disciples to teach them to pray with what is commonly known as "the Lord's Prayer." He then expands on the virtue of persevering in prayer:

> "Ask and it will be given to you; seek and you will find; knock and the door will be opened to you. For everyone who asks receives; he who seeks finds; and to him who knocks, the door will be opened.
>
> Which of you fathers, if your son asks for a fish, will give him a snake instead? Or if he asks for an egg, will give him a scorpion? If you then, though you are evil, know how to give good gifts to your children, how much more will your Father in heaven give the Holy Spirit to those who ask him!"
>
> Luke 11:9–13

This passage presents two unexpected contrasts: a snake instead of a fish, and a scorpion instead of an egg. But that is precisely the nature of the dramatic surprise that awaits those who have lived for themselves by the power of their will for their own sake. You ask for pleasure, and you end up empty. You ask for purpose, and you end up ravaged. In his goodness, God will never betray us into a false hope. He promises to give the Holy Spirit to those who simply and sincerely ask him for that gift of God. If the will to serve God is there, the Holy Spirit must both prompt the prayer and empower the will.

It took two years of struggling with my newfound faith before I understood what it meant to crucify the flesh and to ask the Holy Spirit in persevering prayer to make his home within me. I believe that this is both a moment in time when we make this commitment and a daily reminder to the self of the Spirit's power, which is needed afresh. With that power within, we do the will of the One who sends us.

Being before Doing

In a world that always wants to *do*, we hardly know what it is to *be*. What does it mean to "be"?

When someone asks, "Who are you?" we invariably answer by giving our name. When Moses asked God in Exodus 3 why he was chosen for the task when nothing in him merited the position, God said to him, "I will be with you" (verse 12). Moses immediately responded by asking God what he should say when the Israelites ask him the name of the one who sent Moses to them. God gave an answer in relation to time and existence. He told Moses that he is the eternal "I AM." That defining description stands in contradistinction to the entire created order. No one else can say that he or she is the eternal "I AM."

This is why we always give our names in relationship to somebody else. In my name is my father's name. In my passport is my citizenship. Our identity is locked into place when we come to be, because there was a time when we were not. Time, contingency, and name give us our identity. All are in a relational frame of description. Pilate wondered if Jesus truly was the "Son of God" (see John 19:7–8). In his farewell words to the disciples, Jesus said he was returning to the Father (John 20:17). Who we are is always defined by "whose" we are first. A "Christian" is really "a Christ One." My name is identified with his name. That's what it means.

One of the strangest incidents to hit the news in recent memory was the story of young Whitney Cerak. I received the news of the tragedy that had struck Taylor University in Upland, Indiana, shortly after it happened. Because my son graduated from Taylor and two former Taylor students serve on our staff, we were in a direct line of information about what had happened.

On that fateful day, April 26, 2006, several Taylor students and staff members were making their way back to the campus in a college van when an errant truck hit them head-on. Four students and one staff member died instantly. Funerals were held, and the bereaved mourned their losses. One can only imagine the grief that so many endured through a jolt as sudden and tragic as this. The VanRyn family received word that their daughter, Laura, though seriously injured and in a coma, had survived the crash—the only student still alive. The entire family rushed to the hospital and kept watch over their daughter day and night. The crash had critically injured and disfigured her.

As the days went by, Laura began to open her eyes and then gradually speak. Her family's hearts leaped with joy at the progress she was making. But then some odd doubts began building over some of the things she said. Her young fiancé also felt perplexed and started raising some questions. Reassuring themselves, they attributed all of it to her head injuries and a lengthy recovery time. But when they called her by name, she kept shaking her head and saying her name was not Laura, but Whitney. Oddly enough, there had been a Whitney in the van, but she had been one of those immediately killed. Her family had already buried her. What were they to make of all of this? Why did she keep referring to herself as Whitney as her parents were calling her Laura?

After comparing dental records, officials uncovered a huge blunder. Someone at the scene had falsely identified the lone student survivor as Laura. In fact, Laura VanRyn was dead. The young woman in the rehabilitation center was not Laura, but

Whitney Cerak. The rehab center instantly notified the Cerak family of the mistake. Authorities exhumed the body of the girl mistakenly identified as Whitney and quickly determined from DNA testing that the body was that of Laura VanRyn.

One can only imagine the trauma and the shifting emotions among the families. A family that thought their daughter was dead found out she was actually alive, while a family that had rejoiced in the survival of their daughter discovered that she had died at the crash scene. In an odd way, Whitney will have the privilege of hearing what others said at her "funeral." For one family, at least, there were tears mixed with joy. Explanation after explanation followed to apologize for the colossal mistake. Thoroughly embarrassed, the coroner announced that he was retiring at the end of 2006.

Why does a mistake like this so traumatize us? It does so because we derive our identity from relationship. We carry within us a deep-seated bond to those we love and know and represent. It means something more than just my own individual life. I cannot simply be me without connections and repercussions. Our society is gradually seeing these bonds loosen as we continue to define ourselves in isolation.

Who am I? What does it mean to "be"? The answer is this: I am a child of God related to my heavenly Father. I must be this child in my own understanding. I am not my own. I belong to him. Resting in that knowledge, I know what it is to be his. I should pursue doing God's will, then, and by his grace he will enable my will.

Convictions without Compromise

The will is both the framer of my convictions and the efficient cause in honoring these convictions. Setting these convictions in place gives me guidelines regarding where to draw the lines. Sometimes, unfortunately, we operate within a zone where the lines get blurred—something like the strike zone in baseball where the umpire makes a judgment call on whether it should be a ball or a strike. This is why the broad category of setting life's purpose first and then measuring each moment by this purpose is so important.

The classic example here is Joseph in the Old Testament. When Potiphar's wife repeatedly tempted him, he gave her a pointed answer: "How then could I do such a wicked thing and sin against God?" (Genesis 39:9). Notice that he did *not* say, "What if we get caught?" He did *not* say, "This is a tough call." Any other answer could have left room for her to talk him into the affair. His response removed any possible enticement to rationalize and give in to the temptation.

A conviction is not merely an opinion. It is something rooted so deeply in the conscience that to change a conviction would be to change the very essence of who you are.

Discipline without Drudgery

Hardly anyone likes the word "discipline." It is both the blessing and the bane of our lives. Discipline always seems like a weight around our necks. But if one can only see the need for and the fruit of discipline, one can understand why it offers such great rewards. Think of the athlete who disciplines his or her body for the big race. Think of the discipline of study before an exam and the rewards of success. Think of the labor of love and the victory of reaping a harvest after sowing healthy seeds. Think of honoring God with everything you have and the peace that it brings. The Lord tells us that he disciplines those he loves (see Hebrews 12:6; Revelation 3:19); by implication, then, the undisciplined life is an unloved life.

One Final Warning

There remains one major warning to be stated about the will. It is this: the more one surrenders convictions and neglects discipline, the more one gradually changes one's own hungers and desires. There is an old adage that says, "When you sow a thought you reap an act; when you sow an act you reap conduct; when you sow conduct you reap character; when you sow character you reap a destiny." History is full of faltering wills that have reshaped the future with immeasurable impact. Let's examine just one illustration.

When David was battling the Philistines, he felt terribly homesick and wished he could have a single drink of water from his well in Bethlehem. Three of his choicest warriors in a cloak-and-dagger operation got behind enemy lines and stealthily reached the well. They filled a pitcher they had brought with them for the purpose and stole back out, unnoticed, returning to the place where David was, wishing he could be home. One can imagine the inner thrill they felt as they approached him. They took the pitcher out from under their cloaks, poured out a goblet of water, and said, "Here, David—all the way from your well in Bethlehem." But David paused. When he realized that they had risked their lives to get him that one drink of water, he took the goblet and, in a dramatic illustration, poured the water onto the ground, saying that he could not accept a gift that had jeopardized the lives of others in order to bring him delight. The soldiers were left speechless (see 2 Samuel 23:15–17).

It was a noble act on the part of the king. As I read it, I wondered, "What would have happened if David had reacted the same way when he saw Bathsheba?" The answer is that much of Old Testament history would have changed. But sadly, David's will failed him that time, and the consequences for him and others were disastrous.

We can each recall moments like this in our own lives—moments when our response should have been different from what it was.

A disciplined life that leads to the power to say no eluded David. That one choice led him to make other choices that were devastating to a compromised life and created an appetite for all the wrong things. G. K. Chesterton once said that there are many angles at which you can fall and only one angle at which you can stand straight. The next time you think about the power of your will, think not just of the immediate choice but of all the other compromises to which one ill-advised choice could lead.

CHAPTER 7

Your Worship Matters

THE OLD ANGLICAN MARITAL VOWS INCLUDED A FASCINATING LINE: "With my body, I thee worship." I remember hearing these words as a younger man and inwardly chuckling at the thought. I chuckled because I never realized how beautiful and how profound these words really are.

How does a husband worship his wife with his body? I'm sure you recall the words of the tempter to Jesus: "All this I will give you, ... if you will bow down and worship me" (Matthew 4:9). What an incredible statement for the less powerful to make to the all-powerful! He could have meant it in only one sense: "Change your worship, and I will change the meaning and purpose of things." In fact, that is exactly what he had in mind.

In effect, Satan was declaring, "You look at the world as a possession; I will make it an owner. You look at pleasure as having limits and for the benefit of others; I will make it unconditional and self-serving. You look at life as essential; I will make it existential. You look at yourself as someone under authority; I will make you autonomous." All of Satan's promises were lies, but with the power of the eye and the seduction of the moment, he laid his scheme. He had but a single purpose: to transfer worship from God to himself.

You and I simply cannot serve two masters. Even the devil knows that. Here is life's essential purpose—to worship God in spirit and in truth (see John 4:24). All other purposes are meant to be secondary. When they become primary, they destroy the individual.

The Binding Thread

An old story out of India told of a wealthy man who came into a small village to buy it. Hut by hut, shack by shack, he bought every square inch of the village, except for what belonged to one old man, who refused to sell his hut in the center of the village. The rich man doubled his offer, but the old man refused. He doubled it again, but the old man still refused.

"How much do you want?" the rich man finally asked. "Ask anything and I'll give it to you."

"I'm not selling it at any price," came the reply. "It's mine." The rich man tried and tried to find something the old man would take for his hut, but all his efforts failed. The rest of the village was his, but he could not own the old man's hut.

After some time, the rich man brought his friends to the village to show them what he had bought. As they passed through the center of the village, the old man stepped out of his hut. "Psst. Psst," he beckoned one of the rich man's friends aside. "I hope he isn't telling you that he owns this whole village, because he doesn't. This hut right in the middle belongs to me. This little part right here is mine."

In the same way, all too often the enemy of our souls taunts us in our worship of God: one little part of us still belongs to someone other than God.

This thread of worship binds together all the rest of the threads in the design of our lives. We cannot see the pattern if this thread goes missing. If this thread breaks, the whole design falls apart. If this thread is absent, nothing holds the design to-gether when it comes under stress or gets strained by tension.

You may remember the story of Daniel in the lions' den, told to us in Daniel 6. King Darius had issued an order throughout the nation that for thirty days, anyone found praying to anyone or anything other than the king would be sentenced to death. Daniel did not comply. He refused to rationalize that the order would remain in effect for only thirty days. He rejected the pragmatic decision that he could further his career if he com-plied. He simply would not bow down to any being other than God.

Worship is exclusionary. You cannot compromise on worship.

Worship Defined

What exactly does "worship" mean? The Bible uses several words to describe worship, but the two key terms mean "to bow down" and "to serve." They appear in the same verse on only one occasion, when Jesus responds to Satan after the third temptation: "Away from me, Satan! For it is written: 'Worship the Lord your God, and serve him only'" (Matthew 4:10). Plainly put, worship means "reverence and action." Why is this so important? It's vital because it puts everything else in life into perspective. Worship is coextensive with life. Worship is ultimately "seeing life God's way." Three principal realities combine in worship: mystery, community, and liturgy.

The Mystery of Worship

It is unfortunate that speaking of the possibility of "mystery" and using the term "mystic" leave our pragmatic bent unsatis-fied. "Mysticism" has become a bad word because it smacks of escapism. We think of the mystic as a dreamer, sitting alone atop a mountain somewhere and thinking of nothing all day long. And truthfully, sometimes this is the case. Some Westernized gurus who buy into the marketing philosophy of the West (while supposedly peddling something from the East) thrive on persuading people that their goal should be to empty themselves of all empirical thought.

A very famous guru in India is seeing his empire grow by leaps and bounds as tens of thousands seek an audience with him. Someone I know, a very successful businessman, accompanied a group that had an audience with him. He told me that he sat there for an hour, listening and watching, completely perplexed as to what made this man's teaching and personality so spiritual and powerful. It mystified him because nothing the guru said made any sense, and his behavior seemed juvenile. The guru kept repeating, "Your hands must be full and your head empty. Your hands must be full and your head empty." That was the mantra—empty-headed and full-handed. Newspapers overflow with this man's one-liners. It is all such hocus-pocus that you wonder who has lost sanity—the guru or the media that shower such accolades on him.

If you were to ask the guru what is so revolutionary about his message, in all seriousness he would answer, "A new technique in breathing." So all our "Western maladies" and the world's perplexities would shrink to nothingness if only we breathed with a new technique. What does one say to such gullibility, to such a reductionistic way of thinking?

But behind the crassness, the chants, and the formulas lies an underlying tug—the tug of mystery and the mystical. The truth is that when we lose mystery, our worship becomes merely a grocery list of actions and pronouncements.

The Trinity

What is the mystery so inherent in Christian worship? I believe it is the worship of the holy Trinity in the reverential taking of the elements in the Lord's Supper. In that act, every sense converges. I'll discuss the Lord's Supper in the upcoming section "The Liturgy of Worship" (see page 140). Here I want to briefly consider the Trinity.

God is a Trinity—three Persons in one essence. This is the truth recognized in the historic Christian faith. But how is this even possible? Is this not sheer illogic at work?

It would be if there were three gods. It would be illogical if they were one and three in the same sense. Fishermen, accountants, doctors, rabbis, and homemakers in Jesus' day knew how to differentiate one from three. Peter, James, and John were fishermen. Matthew was an accountant. Luke was a doctor; Paul, a rabbi; and Mary and Martha were homemakers. What made them connect with this profound teaching? They must have recognized a complexity within the very person of God who had revealed himself as a Being in relationship. There was an "I" and a "you" and a "him" within the one essence of the Godhead.

God spoke before creation. God was love before creation. None of these descriptions would make sense if there were not community and unity in the diversity of the Trinity. Is it really impossible for One who was virgin born to be of one essence in a "Tri-unity" within that essence? The prophet said, "For to us a child is born, to us a son is given" (Isaiah 9:6). The Son wasn't born; the child was born. The Son eternally existed.

Even in logic, you see how with each added dimension, the possibilities of the simple become complex while still retaining the simple underpinnings. In one dimension you get a straight line. In two dimensions you get figures. In three dimensions you get objects. With the dimensions of the eternal and the infinite and the uncaused, to conceive of God as one essence and three persons is not unfathomable. It legitimately stays within the realm of mystery.

Not only that, it answers the greatest philosophical question of all time: How does one find unity in diversity when both are realities? The answer is that unity and diversity exist in the

created order because unity and diversity exist in the community of the Trinity, the first cause. This is why Jesus our Lord,
in his final prayer, asked that we as his followers would also
find oneness within the body of Christ (see John 17:20–23).

I realize that to push the very person of God into some ana-
lytical framework runs the risk of "touching the ark of the covenant" (see Numbers 4:15). We must be very, very cautious here.
Yet, God himself invites us to seek an understanding of who he
is. And so, I wonder about what the image of God means. The
Bible tells us that God created male and female in his image
(see Genesis 1:27). This is one of those huge statements about
which we understand so little, so let me probe a bit.

After God created man, he called his creation good, but declared that Adam should not be alone (see Genesis 2:18). In a
real sense, Adam wasn't alone; he was in fellowship with God.
So God must have been saying that Adam lacked a complementary entity that, if present, would give the man the possibility of
full expression. That entity was "woman." God created another
entity so unique and complementary to man that he made possible the kind of fellowship our physicality demanded.

Now carry this to the next step. Together Adam and Eve
fell. Together they felt ashamed. Together they tried to shift
the blame. Together they were offered redemption, and together they would procreate. That togetherness was the setting
in the creation and in both the fall and redemption.

After some time goes by, we move into the time of Abraham. From one father came the two brothers, Isaac and Ishmael. Abraham and Sarah were both involved in the birth of
these boys. Today, the descendants of those two brothers have
unleashed havoc on the world through different beliefs and different worldviews.

Centuries later, when Jesus died on the cross, all of humanity carried the guilt of his crucifixion. After Jesus rose from the
dead, he joined two dejected disciples on the Emmaus road.

They felt despondent because they had hoped that Jesus would deliver them from their political enemies, but Jesus had disappointed them by dying. Everything in that conversation between Jesus and the Emmaus travelers had to do with God's plan in history. They did not know the explanation was coming from Jesus himself. Slowly their eyes were opened to God's plan, that he had a purpose in history and that the design of history pointed to Jesus as the centerpiece. Every power, every hinge on which history pivoted, involved God's plan. These two disciples felt so overcome by it all that they pleaded with him to stay and explain more to them. He stayed, but they did not expect the explanation he gave them at dinner. The manner in which he broke bread opened up their minds and their souls. *God* was breaking bread with them! They instantly recognized the bread as the symbol of Jesus' broken body—broken for all of them (see Luke 24:13–35).

Worship as Community

What begins within me as an individual must continue within me as part of a community. The Christian community is meant to be a healing community.

Some years ago, I read an article by sociologist Daniel Yankelovich about America's search for answers. In his opening lines, he quoted another sociologist's definition of culture: "Culture ... is the effort to provide a coherent set of answers to the existential situations that confront all human beings in the passage of their lives." He then defined a cultural revolution as "a decisive break from the shared meanings of the past."[1]

This is a significant description. "Shared meanings of the past"—is this not what describes a family? A family has shared meanings of life as these meanings unfold in this microcommunity. Have you ever felt like an outsider in some situation because somebody made a quip that you didn't understand but it made everybody else laugh? Then someone says, "Sorry—inside joke." The joke makes reference to some experience shared by others. Now apply this idea to every detail of success and deep disappointment—that is what a family shares. The shared hurts and victories—that's what makes a family a family. All are familiar with the other's needs and feelings. This is a "community."

The church is supposed to be a community—and a healing community at that. Yet if you listen to the stories of disappointment among people within this community, you quickly realize how far from God's purpose and ideal we have drifted.

I'll illustrate this point with a personal, even intimate, anecdote. Some years ago, I seriously injured my back, and as time went on, it became evident that I could not avoid surgery. After many consultations, we set the date and place. I was to have two fusions of my lumbar vertebrae—L3 and L4, and L4 and L5. I had a few other conditions (congenital stenosis and bone spurs inside the vertebrae) that also had to be corrected during surgery.

The procedure took five hours, and then I was wheeled over to the recovery room. Within twenty-four hours, the pain began to build, as expected. By the second day, I was supposed to be changing positions regularly. Of course, with the surgical wound so fresh, I needed help each time I turned. It took two orderlies to help me turn over, and even then they had to use a special technique involving a sheet.

Late on the second night, I needed to turn from my back to my side, so I hit the call button to summon help. A nurse not familiar to me had just come on. I asked her to please send for a couple of strong people to help me.

"Oh, I can do it myself. It's not that difficult," she replied.

"No, ma'am," I said, "I really do need a couple of orderlies because I'm in quite a bit of pain, and I need it done very carefully."

"I've been a nurse for many years. I know what I'm doing," came the impatient retort. Faster than I could even anticipate, she plunged both her hands under my back—and I nearly passed out from the pain. She roughly withdrew her hands and said, "What's all that padding you have on your back?"

"It's the surgical site!" I said, terribly upset with her.

"I thought you had a hip replacement," she said. "I didn't know you had back surgery!"

By this point, the tears had begun to flow, and I had nothing more to say to her. She promptly left the room to go find the orderlies. When I told the doctor about this incident the next day, he was outraged. His job was to mend. The nursing staff was supposed to assist the healing process and aid in the recovery, yet this nurse didn't even know the nature of my injury. How could she be of any help in the healing process?

I couldn't help but think of my younger years in ministry when I carelessly uttered words of castigation against certain persons, things, and behavior, acting like that nurse as I plunged verbal blades into already sore spots. It's so easy to lash out and cut and condemn with prophetic zeal. Pulling someone down is easy; building someone up is difficult. It takes a mature and patient heart to heal with a tender touch without compromising one's convictions.

Was that not the way our Lord handled the Samaritan woman and the woman with the alabaster ointment (see John 4; Matthew 26:6–13)? Without justifying their mistakes, Jesus brought hope and healing, not condemnation and reprimand. But we tend to focus on each other's mistakes and sins. We hurt and injure the already injured. We knock out the already knocked down. We have lost the shared meanings of pain, and so the shared meanings of victory become occasions for jealousy.

The community of the early church—the one that shared everything and held all things in common—(Acts 2:44) did not last long. Over time, jealousies and insensitivities won the day, and they went from "see how they love one another" to division and comparing gifts and demonstrating feelings of superiority over others.

"Comm-union" and "comm-unity" do not ignore diversity. Diversity is recognized and valued, as in the Godhead, but the diversities are brought together because of what all hold in common, namely, the worship of the triune God and the shared meanings of the family of God. The members of a community come together in communion to worship, with their individual lives attuned, first and foremost, to God. Only then can their joint expression take on certain beneficial forms.

The Liturgy of Worship

The book of Acts gives us the five main components of worship: the Lord's Supper, teaching, prayer, praise, and giving. I'll take a brief look at each one in turn.

The Lord's Supper

Worship very plainly opens up the healing of all of mankind. The struggle of gender, the struggle of race, the struggle of history, the struggle to find political liberation, the struggle of our own contradictions—nothing can be mended until we understand the symbol of Jesus' breaking of the bread and pouring of the wine.

You see, when Adam and Eve fell, a rupture occurred between humanity and God. When Cain murdered his brother Abel, and when Isaac and Ishmael warred against each other, man broke away from his fellowman. The Trappist monk Thomas Merton once said, "We cannot be at peace with others because we are not at peace with ourselves, and we cannot be at peace with ourselves because we are not at peace with God."[2] In short, the break of communion with God caused our break with one another, even within the same family. Brokenness well describes the human condition.

Humanity will never find unity until it can understand the reason for that brokenness and the expression of Jesus' broken body and shed blood: "this is my body given for you"; "this cup is the new covenant in my blood, which is poured out for you" (Luke 22:19, 20). Jesus was broken so that we might be mended. "Eat the bread, drink from the cup" is an expression of renewed fellowship with God from which we begin renewed fellowship with our fellow human beings. While baptism is an individual thing as a witness to the world, taking part in the Lord's Supper is a communal thing that expresses within a community the fellowship to which we are all called. The church will never culminate worship until the Communion cup has been drunk to the last dregs. And finally the day will come when we drink from that cup together in heaven. The oneness of the Trinity and the oneness of our communion with the triune God give us the only hope that our fractured lives and fractured societies and races may one day come together.

When Jesus first explained to the disciples what the elements of the Communion represented, many of them could not handle the crudities of the symbolism. And Paul tells us that a person brings harsh judgment on himself or herself by taking part in Communion without first discerning the essence of and implications for that expression (see 1 Corinthians 11:27–29). Worship is consummated in the broken body and the shed blood. This understanding cannot be adulterated. It is exclusive. This is why in the marriage vows the man said, "With my body, I thee worship." He was vowing an exclusive relationship. This is why a man "worships" the body of his spouse. The relationship is sacred, for the two have now been made one flesh. This is why marriage is an expression of worship.

This is also why we commune with the living God as he comes and indwells us. This is why we partake of the broken body and the shed blood, because we bring unity and diversity within us when we worship God in spirit and in truth. Speaking of the overwhelming sense of awe and commission after participating in his first Communion, Thomas Merton wrote:

> I left the altar rail and went back to the pew where the others were kneeling like four shadows, four unrealities, and I hid my face in my hands. In the temple of God that I had just become, the once eternal and pure sacrifice was offered up to the God dwelling in me. The sacrifice of God to God. Now, Christ born in me, a new Bethlehem, and sacrificed in me his new Calvary, and risen in me: offering me to the Father, in himself, asking the Father, my Father and his, to receive me into his infinite and special love—not the love he has for all things that exist, for mere existence is a token of God's love, but the love of those creatures who are drawn to him in and with the power of his own love for himself.[3]

Merton states the mystery of Communion so well. It takes me back to my younger days growing up in India. My parents belonged to a high Anglican church that met in the cathedral in Delhi. I recall watching Communion happen. (I say it in those words because of its formality.) In truth, the actual procedure of Communion left me both a witness and a stranger. I had not yet been confirmed, so I could not participate. Sundays were my cricketing days. So I would keep an eye on the clock to make sure we got out as soon as church ended. I even memorized some of the words of the liturgy just so that I could estimate how long it would be until the supplicants would be called up to receive the bread and the cup. I remember hoping the lineup wouldn't be too long. Row by row the pews would empty as the worshipers went to the altar. I would hear the murmurs of words coming from the ministers as they offered the bread and cup. I had no idea what they were saying or why they were saying it. I watched my mother check her sari so that it was properly draped over her head before she exited the pew to go to the altar and kneel. My dad would have a very solemn expression on his face. As soon as they had partaken of the bread and cup, they would return to the pew and kneel for a few moments—and then we could leave!

Merton's words—"went back to the pew where the others were kneeling like four shadows"—offer a profound description of my whole experience, which to me felt like a shadow. Even in my ignorance, with nothing explained, I felt there was something of a shadow in what was happening and something of reality. It seems appropriate to borrow from Plato's allegory of a cave and apply it here—seeing only shadows on the wall, a phenomenal glimpse, while that elusive "noumenal" and unknowable world of reality yet existed.[4]

Isn't it odd how, whatever our faith and belief may be, we sometimes come to the edge of an idea as though we are about to enter something extraordinary and real, but at the last moment we turn our backs and walk away? I recognized something of divine mystery in Communion, yet I never dared to ask about it because the "reality" of a cricket match seemed too bright for my eyes to ignore. Meanwhile, the murmurings and ritual in the cathedral seemed just a shadow. I missed it, and in the process I missed the cohesion it could have brought to me in that drought-stricken time of my life.

After Merton observes how everything within him converged—Bethlehem, Calvary, and the empty tomb, now all within him; God offering himself to God within the mortal frame of this kneeling man—he ends with the key words "the love of those creatures who are drawn to him in and with the power of his own love for himself." The love with which God himself is bound, now binding us to himself. This is the mystery, the majesty, and the grandeur of holy Communion—God's love shed in our hearts to keep us from fragmentation and dissolution.

In creating Eve for Adam, God intended an exclusive and sacred fellowship. In creating different races, God intended a sacred respect and fellowship. When we eat the bread and drink from the cup with a fellow human being, everything that divides us is overcome by the love that God has within himself. A man who dishonors his wife has broken fellowship with God. A man who dishonors his neighbor has broken fellowship with God. Communion is both vertical and horizontal.

Teaching

The move from Old Testament times to New Testament times saw a dramatic shift in the manner and means of worship. In particular, a shift occurred from the extensive emphasis on ceremony to a focus on teaching. This shift already had begun in the Diaspora, since the Jewish community had to make some changes in worship when the temple became inaccessible.

When we look at the five components of worship, we notice very quickly why teaching became the backbone of the entire worship liturgy. Without the teaching, the rest of the components become prone to heretical expressions. It is the teaching that guides and guards the integrity of worship. It is the teaching that gives understanding of how to be a worshiping community and calls us to remember how God has led in the past. It is the teaching that makes it possible to prepare the children of the community to understand their faith and to pass it on to the next generation.

Some years ago, I was speaking at a conference on the theme of discipleship. I will never forget what happened during the final evening. The week had gone well, and the speakers had addressed their themes with great commitment and expository skill. The final worship service was intended to bring the theme of discipleship to a climax. I was to speak, and then the bishop was to preside over the Lord's Supper. The praise team had occupied the stage for most of the evening. Everything on the platform had been cleared off so that the microphones and instruments could be placed appropriately. When my time came, I did my part (after someone managed to find a lectern on which I could place my notes) and then brought my message to an end. Now the time came to celebrate the Lord's Supper.

But first the table for Communion had to be positioned— and with such little room on the platform, it was difficult for anything to feel liturgically comfortable. After the reading of a portion of Scripture, the bishop took the bread to break it. Finding no good spot on which to place his Bible, he placed it on the floor. While the ushers were distributing the bread, somebody's cell phone rang—no one knew whose it was until it went off again. It belonged to one of the Communion stewards. Pausing from her distribution of the bread, she scurried to the front of the auditorium to turn off her phone. By the time the worship concluded that evening, this experience had supplied a potent symbol of what has happened to the church.

Somewhere, somehow, we have been led to believe that music is the centerpiece of worship. It isn't. It is included in "praise," one of *five* expressions of worship. The clearing of the platform in order to accommodate the musicians and the dis-placement of everything else in order to facilitate the music set would lead us to believe that because we have sung, we have worshiped. We haven't—not necessarily anyway.

I saw this tragic displacement underscored yet again when I spoke in 2004 at the one hundredth anniversary of the Welsh Revival. We were gathered in a historic church, filled with mem-ories of the famed preaching of Evan Roberts, whose ministry had triggered the revival. The Welsh can sing, and did they ever sing! It was worth attending just to see them sing, let alone hear them sing. The signature song of the Welsh Revival—"Here Is Love Vast as the Ocean"—rang out beautifully. It deeply moved me. Whenever I hear the strains of that song, I find it hard to restrain the tears. It almost seems as though the song was written under the inspiration of the Holy Spirit to memorialize the gentle moving of God on the hard hearts of the Welsh mining community and on the larger Welsh population. Yes, it set the Welshmen singing, and it stirred our souls.

But by now, one hundred years had gone by. I met people in that church who said they had not been to church in more than twenty-five years. I saw men and women greeting one another with surprise, not having seen each other in a generation. Oddly enough, the songs remained—but the teaching had vanished.

Can this happen in our time? Is it possible for us to be so swept up by the music and the art of worship that we lose the message and the guidelines on how to worship? Teaching must become the center of worship again, and the ideas that shape our expressions must be biblically induced and shaped. I am not for a moment suggesting that right teaching will guarantee a throbbing, lively church. It may not. But I am suggesting that displaced and misplaced teaching will guarantee a heretical church.

If you do not believe that the situation today has become precarious, stop and ask a young person in your church to take a Bible and show you from Scripture the path of salvation. Ask the same person to name the top choruses or songs, however, and he or she probably will feel very comfortable doing so.

Prayer

In our understanding of prayer, I fear we take one finger of it and think we have the whole fist. Years ago, I heard a story about the well-known Indian Christian mystic Bakht Singh. As he and his associate walked many miles to a conference where he was to speak, a Hindu stopped Bakht Singh and challenged him. "We are in a drought, and you say that God answers prayer. If your God really exists, why don't you ask him right now to send us rain?" Bakht Singh is said to have responded, "If I pray for rain and God answers, will you become a follower of

Jesus?" The man took on the dare and said that he would. As Bakht Singh was about to kneel down in the dust, his assistant placed his hand on his shoulder and said, "Do you really think you should be praying now, when we still have miles to walk and didn't bring our umbrellas with us? Why don't you wait until we reach our destination?"

The first time I read that story, I chuckled. Even today, I do not know whether the story is truth or legend. But true or not, it developed because of Bakht Singh's reputation as such a persuasive prayer warrior that people had implicit faith in his prayers.

A neighbor in New York once came to our home to ask me to pray for an urgent need in her family. "You know," I said to her, "*you* can pray just as easily, and I will help you learn how to pray."

"Oh, that isn't necessary," she replied. "I can pray all I want, but you have an 800 number to God." In other words, I had toll-free, direct access to God, while her prayers, she thought, might be rerouted and thus she couldn't be certain of their destination. Such is the delusion and illusion about prayer we sometimes have. We make it a means to a different end from what God has in mind.

More than anything else, prayer enables you to see your own heart and brings you into alignment with God's heart. Prayer is not a monologue in which we imagine ourselves to be communing with God. Rather, it is a dialogue through which God fashions your heart and makes his dream of you a reality. It is truly the treasured gift of the Christian that through direct answers and not-so-direct answers, the follower of Jesus begins to love God for who he is, not for what he may get out of him.

Praise

Why did God institute festivals and special seasons to assist his people in their worship? For one thing, he did it so that the vast design of his truth could find emphasized expressions at certain times of the year. God designed all of this to help us recall the many threads that go into our worship — celebrating our redemption, commemorating the path to our salvation, exalting in the resurrection.

These diverse particulars converge in unity in God's plan for our redemption, all the way to our heavenly dwelling. Praise has a rich tapestry and when rightly understood, it fills our lives with God's wonder. The loss of worshipful praise results in the defacing of life's essential purpose.

The last book of the Old Testament, the book ascribed to the prophet Malachi, portrays a sad people who had lost the beauty of praise and worship. Every assertion God makes of his love for them, they question. They plead ignorance of any knowledge of God's intervention on their behalf. They even describe their journey with God as burdensome (see Malachi 1:13). That had to be the ultimate insult — that the finite had found the Infinite boring, that the creature had found the Creator insufficient! This is precisely what happens when worship and praise lose their focus and purpose.

Giving

Finally, from the weariness of prayer and praise, the community of the Israelites lost its heart for giving. Instead of offering their best to God, they brought the lame and the blind and the sick — presenting their leftovers to God (see Malachi 1:7 – 14).

To consume the best for yourself and give the crumbs to God is blasphemy. A heart that truly worships is a heart that gives its best to God in time and substance. A heart that truly worships God gives generously to the causes of God — causes that God cares deeply about. I have to wonder whether someday we may wake up to discover that all our incestuous spending on ourselves and our frantic construction of excessively luxurious places of worship—even as we ignore, for the most part, the hurting and the deprived of the world—filled God's heart with pain. Those of us who have enough must learn the art and the heart of giving if we are to be true worshipers. Spending more and more on ourselves and giving less and less to the world in need may be the very reason few take our mission seriously.

The components of worship are clearly laid out for us if we will but listen. God is the object of our worship and our guide on this journey called life, and our resources should be at his disposal. Only then will we discover true pleasure and real meaning, as we distinguish shadow from reality.

Pulling the Threads Together

The last book of the New Testament—the book of Revelation—pictures the church at worship in the new heaven and the new earth. In this glorious scene, a multitude from every language, tribe, and nation speaks with one voice and one language—the language of the soul—to the glory of God (see Revelation 7:9–17). They focus not on themselves but on the God who created them and saved them. This is when culture finds its most sublime and supreme expression of shared meaning.

During the early days of my ministry, I recall such divergent groups of people responding that it planted in my heart a passion for proclaiming the simple truth in sublime terms. I would like to describe two such incidents that I hope will help to pull the threads together.

The first incident took place when I was speaking in a suburb outside of Boston, although I do not even recall what my topic was. When I invited people at the end of the message to come to the altar and kneel if they desired to turn their lives over to Jesus Christ, one of the first to respond wore a face-obscuring hood. Others came forward at the same time, and so I became aware only of several figures kneeling at the altar.

Later on, I stood in the front, answering private questions, when one of our counselors came up and said, "There's a lady here who wants to talk to you." So I went to the altar and knelt beside her. Her name was Janet. The gentleman who called me to meet with her explained apologetically, "I'm sorry, Ravi, but I didn't even know she was a woman because she had a hood over her head. I put my arm around the person, and when I heard her voice, I suddenly realized I was talking to a woman."

Within minutes, Janet told me her story. She made her living as a prostitute, and she had been on her way to the streets that night for another night's work. She had made the same trek every night for many years. But this time she saw the marquis outside the church that advertised special meetings intended to help answer life's questions. "I'm tired of my life," she told me. "I'm weary of the same old drudgery every night. I even hate the money I make. I have my head covered because I'm ashamed to express how dreadful I feel inside. Please help me."

So there I was, a young man in my twenties, kneeling beside a prostitute, watching God transform a heart from the illusion of peddling pleasure to the realization that there was no pleasure in it—that the greatest pleasure of all, as Thomas Merton had put it (see page 142), was to be part of "[God's] infinite and special love—not the love he has for all things that exist, . . . but the love of those creatures who are drawn to him in and with the power of his own love for himself." What a moment it was for me! I will never forget that night.

The psalms tell us that God fills us with eternal pleasures at his right hand (see Psalm 16:11). Worship is the ultimate pleasure that binds and defines all other pleasures.

The second incident took place in another country and another year. I had just finished lecturing on "Man's Search for Meaning." A student stood up and shouted at me, "Everything in life is meaningless!" We exchanged line for line, and he always came back with the same retort: "Everything in life is meaningless!" Finally I assured him that he could not possibly mean it, for the simple reason that I assumed that he assumed that what he was saying was meaningful—and if what he was saying was meaningful, then everything is not meaningless. On the other hand, if everything was meaningless, what he had just said was meaningless too, and therefore, in effect, he had said nothing.

After a short, pin-drop silence, the audience burst into laughter—an unfortunate response for this student. As I walked out of the auditorium, I still remember so clearly seeing him muttering to himself, repeating my words, "If everything is meaningless, then what I said is meaningless; on the other hand ..." I must admit that I found it a humorous sight.

But something special happened later that night. I spoke at a local church in front of a packed house. At the close of the message, I invited men and women to come to the altar and kneel if they wanted to become followers of Jesus Christ. The first to stand and make his way forward was that same young man who earlier in the day had questioned the very possibility that anything had meaning. I stepped away from the pulpit and knelt beside him. In a strange way, he commented, his questions had betrayed his hunger for meaning. Kneeling now at the altar, he recognized that in the act of submission and worship, even his questions were justified.

Whether we seek ways to find pleasure or answers to the questions of a troubled mind, the solution begins with a willingness to see the sacredness of all of life. It must begin by making life an altar—and at an altar we had dare not lie. It is there that life recognizes the sacred.

And this is why worship is primary, the thread of all threads that pulls the multiple threads of life into a beautiful whole. It is the only way the pattern can hold together. The mystery of worship will always remain, but the majesty of worship will triumph.

CHAPTER 8

Your Destiny Matters

———◆◆◆◆———

MARCH 23, 1979, DAWNED A BEAUTIFUL DAY. I HAD BEEN TRAVELING for a few weeks, and Margie was to join me that day in Atlanta. Margie was twenty-eight years old, and as I picked her up at the airport, she looked lovely. It was rush hour, and we drove straight to the church where I was to preach my last sermon for the week. We were planning to leave the next day for Florida for a week's vacation. We got into the car and headed north on Interstate 85, Atlanta's major artery through the city.

About fifteen minutes into the drive, Margie began to feel a strange pain in her abdomen. As the pain grew, she began to feel weak, and when I turned to look at her, she could barely utter the words, "Please take me to the place where you're staying. I need to lie down." I knew that something was wrong. Soon she began to lose consciousness. I swerved the car to straddle the right lane and the shoulder of the highway and turned on my emergency lights. Incredibly, the traffic began to give me room to reach the exit. I saw a Holiday Inn nearby and sped into the parking lot.

As I struggled to get Margie out of the car, she completely passed out. A woman walking through the parking lot saw my struggle and came to my aid. It seemed as though it took forever, but we got her into the hotel lobby and laid her on a couch.

The woman told me she was a nurse and "just happened" to be coming into the hotel for dinner. She grabbed Margie's wrist to take her pulse—and felt nothing. Nor could she detect any respiration. "She must have had a heart attack!" she exclaimed, and she began to do a heart massage.

"A heart attack?" I wondered aloud. "How can it be a heart attack? She's not even twenty-nine years old yet!"

The receptionist at the front desk immediately telephoned for an ambulance and brought an oxygen tank over to her. Within minutes, we were racing to the hospital. The paramedic at the back of the ambulance with Margie told the driver to pick up speed because he couldn't find a pulse or any blood pressure.

When we arrived at the hospital, everybody was on high alert. Immediately they whisked Margie out of my sight. It seemed like an eternity before the surgeon came out to me and said that they were going to operate immediately. He thought she had an ectopic pregnancy that had ruptured, but because he didn't know for sure, he planned to open up her entire abdomen. And, he said, he might have to do a hysterectomy to save her life.

It seemed like yet another eternity before the surgery ended and the doctor came out to say that Margie would be fine. She had lost over 60 percent of her blood and had required several transfusions. He said that if she had ruptured on the plane or if we had brought her to the hospital ten minutes later, I probably would have been receiving her corpse and not a live body.

When I finally got back to my hotel room at the end of a long night, I was in a daze. Not until I saw the green garbage bag into which someone in the emergency room had put Margie's clothes did it hit me how close I had come to losing her. My brother, a surgeon, phoned me and told me that this was as close a call as one could get; such an emergency has one of the highest mortality rates a hospital ever sees.

Margie and I have reflected on this event numerous times, and I shudder every time I think of it. But the most interesting thing is her recollection of it. Somehow, she knew all the details. She heard the nurse in the hotel lobby diagnose a heart attack. She heard my response and longed to comfort me and tell me that she would be all right, but she couldn't speak. She heard the ambulance attendants speaking and worried that she would feel embarrassed if they found nothing wrong. She said it was as though she were floating against the ceiling, watching the whole episode unfold. She felt no emotion. It felt as though she were watching someone else, having a sort of "out of the body" experience.

One wonders about the true nature of her experience. Was her mind in a state of shock? Did she have a "near death" experience, cut short by intervention? We think about these things and in many ways know so little about the final moments before death and those moments immediately after death. It is highly risky to speculate too much on those "in the body" or "out of the body" moments, but the ideas continue to intrigue us. We wish that we really knew.

When we think of destiny, however, we make a mistake in thinking only of death or what happens after death. Destiny involves much more than this. It is the culmination of all that life was, including how that person prepares for death, whether it comes soon or after several years. Destiny incorporates the sense of purpose and design when it lies in the hands of a sovereign God. We saw in the last chapter how worship pulled together all the threads of our design for the here and now. What does this mean for the hereafter and the eternal?

We Have the Image Given

The Scriptures clearly declare that God has chosen us to be conformed to the image of his Son. The Son has provided the destination we must reach. We will never be like Jesus in essence, but God calls us to be like him in our reflective splendor.

The Old Testament forbade all Israelites from making graven images (see Exodus 20:4). It prohibited everyone from trying to represent God in a physical form. This is a specific command, given for an obvious reason. The means can very easily become the ends. But God has given us the privilege to be his image bearers and to reflect his splendor.

So what splendor are we to reflect?

Do you remember when Jesus' disciples asked him where he lived (see John 2:38)? It was a loaded question. They really wanted to know Jesus' point of origin and what he called home. The first element in reflecting Jesus' image is to understand that *his home was with the Father* (see John 8:14–29; 12:44–50). Jesus talked a great deal about his mission on earth, but as he drew closer to the completion of that mission, he spoke often of returning to the Father, from whom he had come (see John 13:3). Jesus told the disciples that he had prepared a place so that where he was they—and we—could also be (see John 14:2–4). This simple description of being at home with God is the ultimate destiny of the follower of Jesus Christ.

In a mobile society like ours, where economic standing is paramount, home has become a very transient thing. We move from house to house, city to city, and never stay long enough anywhere to call it home. Home becomes where the job is; and the heart, in effect, becomes homeless.

For more than three decades now, I have been an itinerant man, traveling across this globe. I have seen so much, enjoyed so much, been rewarded so much, and been befriended by so many. I have seen the beauty of the Taj Mahal, the majesty of the Swiss Alps, the vastness of the oceans. I have tasted some of the most delicious food that any taste buds could relish. I have heard some of the kindest accolades showered on me by my hosts. I will never forget the delights of these experiences.

But nothing—and I mean *nothing*—thrills my heart more than when a successful trip nears its end and the day comes to pack my bags and head to the airport. That means *I'm going home.*

What is it about home that makes me feel this way? It is the one place in the world where I can be myself and be accepted for who I am. I wish I had been a better father and husband. If I had to do it all over again, I would change some things I did or said. But as much as I regret my foibles and blunders, they have never been held against me. Home is where I wake up and don't need to look perfect in order for my wife to say, "I love you." Home is where I can put up my feet and let my head drop—the heavens know what I look like. But even in that less than ideal state, I may receive a kiss from my wife and experience the warmth as she places a blanket over me. Home means the care and honor given to us while we are unadorned and spent. Home is where I am loved just for who I am, not for my name or how I preach or what books I have written—but just for being me.

This is why I believe our Lord describes our presence with him in heaven as knowing him, even as we are known (see 1 Corinthians 13:12). God knows us in our weaknesses; we will know him in his transcendent majesty. He has always known us for who we really are; yet he calls us his children and his friends. And finally, when all is said and done, he calls us home to be with him. We will be at home with God! That's my destiny (see Revelation 21:3).

In "A Baby's Funeral," F. W. Boreham tells a most tearful story. He writes of the day he and his wife were packing a picnic basket to head out to spend the day in a park by the river. He looked out of his kitchen window and saw a woman pacing the sidewalk outside of his home, looking very troubled and tentative with every step, suddenly turning toward his door with determination and then, just as suddenly, turning away.

After watching her for several minutes, he stepped outside and asked if he could help her.

"Are you the minister of the church nearby?" she asked. When he said he was, she asked if she could come in; she had a sad story to tell. He invited her to sit in a comfortable chair, and he sat opposite her, leaning forward to hear her story. Her baby had died suddenly, she said, and she had rarely gone to church. She wanted someone to help her bury the little one.

"I'd be honored to do it," said Boreham. He asked for all the particulars—the name of the father, the date of birth, and all the information that should be entered into the register. They set the time for the funeral—the next afternoon—and she said good-bye. As Boreham picnicked with his wife that morning, he told her that the woman had seemed terribly distracted the whole time she was at their house. He wondered if there could be more to the story. But then he let the thought go.

When he and his wife returned at sunset, there was the young woman, standing outside the house. "I've not told you the truth," she admitted. "I am not married. My baby was born out of wedlock and was terribly deformed." Sobbing, she proceeded to tell the rest of the story.

"That's all right," he assured her. "None of that ought to affect the funeral tomorrow."

The next afternoon it was just the three of them at the funeral—Boreham, his wife, and the woman. To make matters worse, there was a driving rainstorm, and to add desolation to tragedy, the cemetery was brand-new. This little deformed corpse was the first to be laid into that barren stretch of ground. There they all clutched an umbrella, just the three of them. Boreham said that in all of his years of ministry, he had seldom felt as alone as at that moment. He could only imagine the young mother's ache and fear. As the years went by, however, that mother became one of the most faithful members of that church. Week after week she showed up.[1]

"Why would this woman be so faithful in church attendance?" one might ask. Surely it was because it was there that her baby was received and treasured. In a sense it became her new home, through the death of a beloved little one. It was the place where arms opened to her and became wrapped around her. It was the place where she felt loved and forgiven. It was the gateway to her baby's heavenly journey.

The cemetery, new or old, is not our ultimate destination; it is merely a place in which to remember the symbols of a farewell. The person is not there; only the last memory is there. The respect shown in a cemetery comes not because it is home, but because it is where we bid believing loved ones a temporary good-bye. Jesus came from the Father and returned to the Father to prepare a place for you and for me. *That's* home. *That* is our eternal dwelling. We cherish the tender metaphor of home because there we will unpack our suitcases for the last time.

Touching the Eternal

I believe that something else is crucial as well. Do you recall how fearful the disciples had become after the death of Jesus? They went into hiding, half hoping the story had not yet ended but knowing full well that they had little prospect of any good news (see John 20:19). The women visited the tomb just to pay their respects (see Luke 24:1); not for a moment did they expect to find that the tomb was empty and that Jesus would appear to them there (see Matthew 28:9–10; John 20:14–18).

Naturally, the whole resurrection story became almost fantastic, practically impossible to believe. But the women rushed back at Jesus' instruction to tell the rest of the disciples that Jesus was alive, just as he had promised. This was too much for anyone. The virgin birth was tough enough to accept—but now, the overcoming of death itself? As fast as their feet could carry them, Peter and John ran to check out the story (see John 20:3–9).

As might be expected, people reacted to the risen Jesus in different ways. On the evening of that first day of the week, the disciples met in secrecy behind a locked door, afraid of what had happened and of what might happen still. All of a sudden, Jesus appeared. He did not need an unlocked door. He greeted them with the blessing to be at peace and then commissioned them to go and tell everyone that he was alive and well (see John 20:19–23).

As it happened, Thomas was absent that evening; perhaps the true-blue empiricist figured that it was all over, so there was no need to hang out with the rest of the losers. But the disciples wasted no time telling him what he had missed (see John 20:25).

"No, it simply cannot be," he insisted. "I will not believe it unless I can see Jesus for myself and touch the marks of the nails in his hands and the wound in his side." What a truly odd request. Thomas was the one who earlier had asked Jesus where he was going and how he could join him (see John 14:5). Now Thomas was struggling to believe in Jesus and remained adamant that he needed more than just to see Jesus—he needed to touch the wounds to know their reality.

A week later, the disciples again met in a locked room. This time Thomas joined them. Maybe he thought that if this whole thing was for real, he wasn't going to miss it a second time. I truly wonder what went through the disciples' minds. Did somebody suggest that they not lock the door, just in case Jesus needed to come in? And did someone else say, "It doesn't matter. It was locked the last time"? With predictable fear, they did lock the door—and suddenly their Lord stood in their midst. He spoke first to Thomas: "Put your finger here; see my hands. Reach out your hand and put it into my side. Stop doubting and believe" (John 20:27).

Thomas gave a brief and most appropriate response: "My Lord and my God!" Yes, Jesus had vanquished death. And what was more, though walls and locked doors couldn't restrict Jesus' new body, at the same time, the disciples could see and touch and feel and recognize Jesus for who he was. In the garden of Eden, touching and eating the symbol of good and evil was fatal because it came at the instigation of the devil through the seduction of the eyes for the purposes of the flesh, which resulted in death. Now the Lord invited them to touch in response to their awe at his triumph over the flesh and the vanquishing of death. Taking the fruit of the tree of the knowledge of good and evil was to arrogate to ourselves the right to self-determination. Now the touch of the Creator makes it possible for us to recognize him as the author of our life and destiny.

Of all the sensitivities we have, the sense of touch is the one we long for the most. From the time we are born, we cry for food and for the arms of a loved one around us. A massage therapist friend of mine told me that massage is especially important for older people who live alone—for most of them, it is the only time anyone touches them. A loving touch provides comfort and protection.

One of our most important faculties is the ability to feel, whether in the physical or emotional realm. Our bodies hurt—and we feel pain. We hold a loved one's hand or kiss a beloved face because we feel love. But other feelings come from knowing or imagining something. Good news or bad news, each in its own way, brings a physical response from the body. The chemistry and the physiology of our bodies and our minds respond to the relationship we have with the news bearer or with those the news concerns. Our feelings get in sync with the reality our minds know. The sequence goes like this: reality ⇨ our knowledge of that reality ⇨ our reaction to that reality (our feelings). We know how to gauge a person's normal reaction to a certain reality.

Now, did you notice how academic this discussion began to sound the moment we started to analyze why we feel the way we do? It seems so inappropriate to try to dissect feelings. The old adage holds true that "some things are better felt than 'telt.'" We know why—it is because we are creatures who feel.

One of the most fascinating personalities in the literary world of years gone by was Oscar Wilde, a name synonymous with hedonism and flamboyant living. He became the willing mascot of all who wished to live by the senses and sensuality. Yet, in his early forties, as he lay dying in a small room in Paris, his mind wandered to eternity. He penned "De Profundis," which has had a huge impact on many. In the darkness of his fears he said something fascinating:

> *Out from the mist, the mist, I cry,*
> *Let not my soul in numbness die!*
> *My life is furled in every limb,*
> *And my existence groweth dim.*
> *My senses all like weapons rust,*
> *And lie disused in endless dust.*
> *I may not love, I may not hate,*
> *Slowly I feel my life abate.*
> *Oh, would there were a heaven to hear!*
> *Oh, would there were a hell to fear!*
> *Ah, welcome fire, eternal fire,*
> *To burn forever and not tire!*
> *Better Ixion's whirling wheel,*
> *And still at any cost to feel!*
> *Dear Son of God, in mercy give*
> *My soul to flame, but let me live!*[2]

Wilde begged God not to take away his capacity to feel, even if it was just to burn. No doubt his poetic imagination drove him to such verse, but he made his point. To not feel is to be dead in the truest sense of the term. To feel is to be alive.

What is my destiny? It is to feel, to see, to have all of the senses finally converge in the fullest expression of purpose. Everything I experience and feel before I arrive at that heavenly home amounts to mere analogy. Everything in my heavenly home is consummate expression.

But Is It Real?

Is all of this just fanciful imagination? No, it is reality. We have several hints, both in our experience and in history. Take a look at our experience. Our longings give us a hint of our eternal home and that consummate touch. C. S. Lewis masterfully expressed the longings of the human heart in his essay *The Weight of Glory*:

> In speaking of this desire for our own far-off country, which we find in ourselves even now, I feel a certain shyness. I am almost committing an indecency. I am trying to rip open the inconsolable secret in each one of you—the secret which hurts so much that you take your revenge on it by calling it names like Nostalgia and Romanticism and Adolescence; the secret also which pierces with such sweetness that when, in very intimate conversation, the mention of it becomes imminent, we grow awkward and affect to laugh at ourselves; the secret we cannot hide and cannot tell, though we desire to do both. We cannot tell it because it is a desire for something that has never actually appeared in our experience. We cannot hide it because our experience is constantly suggesting it, and we betray ourselves like lovers at the mention of a name.[3]

How does Lewis describe this constant hinting of something else within ourselves? He compares it to the surprise we feel with the passing of time, even though time is part of our experience. "How time flies," we say. Then Lewis says that such a reaction would be as anomalous as a fish expressing surprise at the wetness of water—unless, of course, it were intended to live on dry land.[4] Those words capture it well. We react to the speed of time because, deep in our souls, we are "created for eternity."[5] Yet we have "a certain shyness" about talking about heaven, perhaps because we feel we are too intellectually advanced for "fairy tales." Nevertheless, deep inside, our longing for heaven suggests its reality, all the time.

The poets do not fear to tackle the subject because imagination gives them license to confess to this longed-for and hinted-at reality. Years ago, I remember hearing the classic poem written by Adelaide Anne Proctor titled "The Lost Chord" (set to music by Arthur Sullivan) and thinking about it in the same way:

> *Seated one day at the organ,*
> *I was weary and ill at ease,*
> *And my fingers wandered idly*
> *Over the noisy keys.*

> *I do not know what I was playing,*
> *Or what I was dreaming then;*
> *But I struck one chord of music,*
> *Like the sound of a great Amen.*

> *It flooded the crimson twilight,*
> *Like the close of an angel's psalm,*
> *And it lay on my fevered spirit*
> *With a touch of infinite calm.*

> *It quieted pain and sorrow,*
> *Like love overcoming strife;*
> *It seemed the harmonious echo*
> *From our discordant life.*

> *It linked all perplexed meanings*
> *Into one perfect peace,*

And it trembled away into silence
As if it were loath to cease.

I have sought, but I seek it vainly,
That one lost chord divine,
Which came from the soul of the organ,
And entered into mine.

It may be that death's bright angel
Will speak in that chord again —
It may be that only in heaven
I shall hear that grand Amen.

Every line in this poem is profound. Consider just these two: "It seemed the harmonious echo / from our discordant life." Even as we live with such discord, our souls get hints of the harmony that we long for and await. Yes, that longing is there. Such writers do not create out of emergency situations, seeing life from a semitranscendent vantage point. They have not lost 60 percent of their blood when they write things such as this. They give us a glimpse of the eternal from a sacred imagination.

But one might well argue that it is still just that—imagination. Wishful thinking! Wishes do not manufacture truth. Wishes do not guarantee fulfillment.

The Body of Evidence

This is where I think that the Christian faith rises to its most authentic. When Lazarus, a friend of Jesus, came down with a serious illness, his sisters Mary and Martha sent for the Master. Before Jesus arrived at their home in Bethany, Lazarus died, and the sisters greeted the Lord with the half-indicting words, "If you had been here, my brother would not have died." Martha added, "But I know that even now God will give you whatever you ask" (John 11:21–22).

What an odd construction of thought. She is really saying, "Since you were not here to keep this tragedy from happening, it is now our expectation that you will reverse it." Jesus did assure her that one day Lazarus's death would be reversed (verse 23). But that was not good enough; Martha wanted it reversed right then. In effect, she was willing to let Lazarus die twice. (I have visited a grave in Cyprus that purports to be the grave of Lazarus. Inscribed on the grave are the words, "Lazarus, Friend of Jesus, Twice Dead.")

In a dramatic move, Jesus went to the tomb. When he saw where his friend lay, Jesus wept (see John 11:35). He wept, even though he knew that, at least for then, he was going to reverse death. Death is powerful, but the power of God to raise us indeed shouts the triumph of love over sin.

Lazarus's resurrection portended what would happen to Jesus himself. And here is the point: if Jesus were a charlatan or had deceived himself, he could have kept his plan going in perpetuity simply by saying, "I will spiritually rise again." Such a claim could never be contradicted or proven false. But Jesus made no such promise. He promised a bodily resurrection—a concretely demonstrable falsehood if it were not to happen. This is vitally important. Jesus made an empirically verifiable claim *and then fulfilled it.* This statement has profound implications. It means that these bodies of ours, which the apostle Paul describes as a "temple of the Holy Spirit" (1 Corinthians 6:19) will some day be transformed to be like [Christ's] "glorious body," just as the Bible declares (Philippians 3:21). They will continue to exist and our individual identities and personalities will be translated into an eternal realm.

The transfiguration of Jesus as described in the Gospels has always fascinated me. Peter, James, and John became eyewitnesses of this staggering event. I find it extraordinary that the disciples who saw Moses and Elijah talking to Jesus immediately recognized those Old Testament heroes. Did they hear more than the voice from heaven? Did Jesus identify the ancient pair? Did God give the disciples an inner disclosure? The Evangelists do not tell us.

Peter had an especially intriguing response to the two visitors: he wanted to put up a shelter for each of them (see Matthew 17:4). A shelter from what? And why would they who lived in heaven wish to have a shelter on earth? It didn't dawn on Peter that Moses and Elijah had no grave markers because God himself had buried Moses and left no marker (see Deuteronomy 34:5–6), while Elijah never died but had relocated directly to heaven in a flaming chariot (see 2 Kings 2:11). Neither had a burial stone. And Jesus himself would need no memorial stone.

The destiny God has for us does away with these things that we deem so important now—shelters, tombs, and gravestones. In the end, our identities will be with God, and our personalities will be sublimely consummated to the purpose designed for each one of us. Our move from earth to heaven will serve as the thread that ties our memories together with reality and will enable us to see the temporal in the light of the eternal.

Johann Sebastian Bach once said that the only purpose for music should be the glory of God and the re-creation of the human spirit. What Bach said of music will one day be seen as true of all of life. We will be "re-created," and all the threads of our earthly life will come together for the design that we will experience in heaven. Every tribe, every language, every moment, every pain, and every sorrow will come together in the consummate pattern of God's design.

Questions Answered

I had a very close friend in my undergraduate days named Koos Fietje—a tall and determined Dutchman, a man with a tender heart and a fearless personality. We shared many hours of friendship and conversation.

Eventually, he and his wife, Colleen, served as missionaries in Thailand. On one occasion while en route to Cambodia, I stopped for a night in Bangkok, and Koos and I talked the whole night long about our dreams and plans to work for God wherever he led us and called us. We prayed together, and after we parted, I could not stop thinking about what Koos had said to me. He felt he would have to pay with his life for his boldness for Christ. Seven years after that conversation, in 1981, Koos Fietje was murdered in the little town in Thailand where he had proclaimed Christ so fearlessly.

More than twenty years went by before I met his daughter, Martina, for the first time. She had come to one of my lectures and had been standing nearby while others took their turn to speak with me for a little while. She then introduced herself. "I've been waiting for a long time to meet you," she said, "because I was told that you were one of my dad's closest friends."

I put my arm around her, and we sat down to talk. She was very little when her father was killed and had never returned to Thailand. She was now a young married woman, but she still felt haunted by memories of her father's death. She wished that some day she could visit his grave in Thailand. I took it upon myself to make her wish come true, and recently our ministry sent Martina and her husband to Thailand. When she returned, she wrote these words to me:

> *Dear Ravi,*
>
> *Dave and I returned from Thailand this week and are overwhelmed by God's graciousness to us during our time there. We are still processing what happened, but I wanted you to know that it was an unforgettable experience. Not only did I visit Dad's grave, but I stood on the spot where he was killed; the lady who had been sitting next to him that night was with me, telling*

me everything that had happened. It was her husband who paid to have him killed. So many questions were answered, but more importantly we were able to witness the impact that my dad had on these people. There are over eighteen churches planted in the area where my parents worked—and even in the village where he was killed we sat with some believers and sang and read the Bible. As we were leaving the believers, they were witnessing to a neighbor lady. It was abundantly clear that the Thai people loved him and twenty years later still miss him terribly. A number of them said they have never had such a bold witness since....

I can't thank you enough for making this happen. Perhaps some day I will be able to share more with you if you are ever in this area again.

Martina's letter deeply moved me. It brought closure to a daughter with regard to the death of her father, but it also opened a door to help her understand the immense impact of a life so faithfully lived.

"Many questions were answered." Yes, but many more will be answered when she sees her dad again in heaven.

"I can't thank you enough for making this happen." No, it was not really me; it was God and his faithful stewards that made it happen. Standing by the grave of her dad with the one whose husband had paid for the murder—what emotions must have surged through her heart! But Koos's grave is not his legacy. The eighteen churches are his legacy, and his memorial is on high.

God may not call many of us to pay for our faith with martyrdom. But we are called to see the gracious hand of a designing God in our lives. We are called to respond to God's nod. He holds the threads. He has given us his promise:

"For I know the plans I have for you," declares the LORD, "plans to prosper you and not to harm you, plans to give you hope and a future. Then you will call upon me and come and pray to me, and I will listen to you. You will seek me and find me when you seek me with all your heart. I will be found by you," declares the LORD.

JEREMIAH 29:11–13

The design is beautiful. The promise is sure. The end result is profound. The answers will all be there. But the condition is clear: we must search for God with all our hearts. And when you are about to walk into eternity, may you also be able to say, as did my father-in-law, "Amazing! It's just amazing!"

Epilogue

———◆·✦·◆———

As I was bringing this book to a close early one morning, I witnessed a vivid illustration of all that I have been trying to say. Sadly, it was not a pleasant experience.

I had just returned from an overseas trip during which I had bought my wife a beautiful necklace of semiprecious stones studded on a gold chain, each gem surrounded by zircons. The colors shone so beautifully that everyone who saw it said they wished they were the ones receiving it. I could hardly wait to present it to Margie. So at just the right moment, when the children were watching, I gave it to her. She loved it and asked me to tell her about the stones that adorned the necklace. That night we got to bed quite late.

I arose early the next day and went to the kitchen to make a pot of coffee. I was intending to begin writing the last chapter of this book. As I walked into the kitchen, I heard some crunching sounds. I looked in the direction of the commotion, and there, in the mouth of the puppy belonging to my daughter, was that beautiful necklace. Already it had been chewed into oblivion.

I must be honest. I just stood there, my eyes filling with tears. What could I do? This little representative of the canine world had absolutely no idea what she was destroying. Evidently she had stood on her hind legs and knocked the necklace down from the desk where my wife had left it. I had no rational way to tell this dog the damage she had done.

The puppy had taken a beautiful, elegantly designed piece of jewelry and treated it like a bone to chew on. It was not just that the dog destroyed something beautiful; worse, she had no understanding of the purpose of a magnificent piece of jewelry. I called my wife and showed her the remains. As she examined it, she thought it could be taken to a jeweler and repaired. (I have to admit that I wondered if there was a place to take the puppy as well. But for the sake of my daughter, I shall not head in that direction. Besides, the thought itself is unkind.)

Just think of the destruction of design in just one small piece of jewelry and how heartsick we feel about the loss. What, then, must be in the heart of God when we see no design and no purpose in our lives? What must God feel when we treat the crown of his creation as something to be consumed rather than something to be loved and admired with reverence? God intends to help each one of us live with his design in mind and not to trample underfoot his exquisite workmanship.

As I mourned the damage to the necklace, I quickly found myself reprimanding myself. You see, the previous night my wife had also just returned from a trip, having spent the weekend with her sisters and some childhood friends. One of those friends had suffered through a difficult few years. Within a short span of time she had lost her father, her husband, and her teenage son. The death of her son was the most sudden and grievous. My wife's friend had told her, "When you lose a child, it suddenly puts all of life in perspective."

So I apply a closing caution to every reader: God wants none of us to perish. He left the ninety-nine sheep safely in the fold to go looking for the single lost one (see Luke 15:3–7). Every one of God's creation, he wishes to preserve. His design for you is the best thing he has for you. Let God hold the threads so that you will someday see the beauty and the marvel he had in mind when he created you.

But there is a second application: if you fail to find this design, the biggest price you may pay is your children or those who look to you as an example. As you let God's design be worked out in you, you will see its impact in others and for generations. Let the tapestry show its beauty. Shun the threadbare existence. God holds the threads; you hold the shuttle. Move it at God's behest, and watch the making of something spectacular.

I close with the words of a beautiful hymn written by Charles Wesley. May it be your prayer, as it is mine.

O Thou who camest from above,
the pure celestial fire to impart;
kindle a flame of sacred love
upon the mean altar of my heart.

There let it for thy glory burn
with inextinguishable blaze,
and trembling to its source return,
in humble prayer and fervent praise.

Jesus, confirm my heart's desire
to work and speak and think for thee;
still let me guard the holy fire,
and still stir up thy gift in me.

Ready for all thy perfect will,
my acts of faith and love repeat,
till death thy endless mercies seal,
and make my sacrifice complete.

Notes

Introduction

1. Quoted in Harold Bosley, *Sermons on Genesis* (New York: Abingdon, 1958), 206.

2. The phrase "dark night of the soul" is taken from the writings of Saint John of the Cross (sixteenth century) and reflects the name of both a poem and a commentary on the poem.

3. Isaac Watts, "Our Frail Bodies, and God our Preserver," in *Hymns and Spiritual Songs*, Book 2, Hymn 19.

Chapter 1: Your DNA Matters

1. William Shakespeare, "Macbeth," Act 5, Scene 5.

2. Quoted in Alistair McGrath, *Glimpsing the Face of God* (Grand Rapids: Eerdmans, 2002), 10.

3. See Richard Doyle, *Jack the Giant Killer* (Everyman's Library Children's Classics; New York: Random House, 2000). An online version can be viewed at *www.authorama.com/english-fairy-tales-21.html* (October 10, 2006).

4. See Plato, *The Republic*, trans. Benjamin Jowett (New York: Collier, 1901), 2:359d–60b.

5. H. G. Wells, *The Invisible Man* (first published in 1897; excerpt from chapter 20 [can be viewed at *www.readprint.com/chapter-10226/H-G—Wells*]).

6. Gary LaFerla, *Finding Your Way: A Guide to Discovering God's Best for Your Life* (Grand Rapids: Baker, 2005), 186–87.

7. C. S. Lewis, *Mere Christianity* (New York: Macmillan, 1952), 86.

Chapter 2: Your Disappointments Matter

1. An online version of this story can be viewed at *www.mainlesson. com/display.php?author=richards&book=windows&story=golden* (October 10, 2006).

2. Calvin Miller, *Spirit, Word, and Story* (Grand Rapids: Baker, 1996), 56–57.

3. Quoted in F. W. Boreham, *Dreams at Sunset* (London: Epworth, 1954), 51.

4. Quoted in Philip Yancey, *Soul Survivor* (New York: Doubleday, 2001), 45.

5. Jim McLean, "The Massacre of Glencoe." Words and music by Jim McLean. Publisher: Duart Music, 1963. Used by permission.

6. William Walsham How, "It Is a Thing Most Wonderful," composed in 1872.

7. Malcolm Muggeridge, *Jesus Rediscovered* (Garden City, N.J.: Doubleday, 1969), 54–55.

Chapter 3: Your Calling Matters

1. Vince Lombardi, "No. 1 Speech." *Vince Lombardi: www. vincelombardi.com/about/speech.html* (October 10, 2006).

2. Quoted in F. W. Boreham, *Temple of Topaz* (New York: Abingdon, 1928), 64.

3. Francis Thompson, "The Kingdom of God," in *Complete Poetical Works of Francis Thompson* (New York: Boni & Liveright, 1913), 356–57.

4. Cited in Os Guinness, *Unspeakable* (San Francisco: HarperSanFrancisco, 2005), 19.

5. Cited in F. W. Boreham, *The Tide Comes In* (London: Epworth, 1958), 69.

6. F. W. Boreham, "The Poppies in the Corn," in *Mountains in the Mist* (Grand Rapids: Kregel, 1995), 278–79.

Chapter 4: Your Morality Matters

1. Kai Nielson, "Why Should I Be Moral?" *American Philosophical Quarterly* 21 (1984), 90.

2. Bertrand Russell, "A Letter to *The Observer*," October 6, 1957.

3. Cited in Philip Novak, *The Vision of Nietzsche* (Rockport, Mass.: Element, 1996), 11.

4. See Alister McGrath, *Glimpsing the Face of God* (Grand Rapids: Eerdmans, 2002), 39–40.

5. See C. S. Lewis, *The Screwtape Letters* (1942; repr., New York: HarperCollins, 2001), 63–67.

Chapter 6: Your Will Matters

1. Cited in Sherwood Eliot Wirt and Kersten Beckstrom, eds., *Topical Encyclopedia of Living Quotations* (Minneapolis: Bethany House, 1982), 227.

2. "David Livingstone—Missionary to Africa." *Moments with the Book:* http://www.mwtb.org/html/410470.html (October 26, 2006).

Chapter 7: Your Worship Matters

1. Daniel Yankelovich, "New Rules in American Life: Searching for Self-fulfillment in a World Turned Upside Down," *Psychology Today* (April 1981), 36.

2. Thomas Merton, *The Living Bread* (New York: Farrar, Straus & Cudahy, 1956), xiii.

3. Cited in Hugh T. Kerr and John Mulder, eds., *Famous Conversions* (Grand Rapids: Eerdmans, 1994), 241.

4. See Plato, *The Republic*, Book VII, 514a–521d.

Chapter 8: Your Destiny Matters

1. F. W. Boreham, "A Baby's Funeral," in *Dreams at Sunset* (London: Epworth, 1954), 51.

2. Cited in F. W. Boreham, *The Heavenly Octave: A Study of the Beatitudes* (Grand Rapids: Baker, 1936), 28.

3. C. S. Lewis, *The Weight of Glory and Other Essays* (Grand Rapids: Eerdmans, 1979), 4.

4. Cited in Sheldon Vanauken, *A Severe Mercy* (New York: Harper & Row, 1977), 93.

5. Vanauken, *A Severe Mercy*, 203.

Appendix: 25 Key Questions

As a Christian apologist who often stands before hostile audiences, I field questions on many topics, ranging from issues of origin to issues of meaning, morality, and destiny. As sophisticated as some of these questions may sound, when they are stripped of excess verbiage, there remains the issue of God's purpose and design for this world and for each individual. Accordingly, for the questions that follow I have focused on the existential side of how the Christian faith deals with these common struggles.

I strongly encourage the reader, Bible in hand, to ponder these questions and, whenever possible, to discuss them in groups. Look for answers that can be sustained by the Scriptures and tested by argument and discussion.

Just as there is a design to each life, there is a design in God's answers. His goal is that his answers will touch both heart and mind.

For those who wish to pursue these questions at a more theoretical and philosophical level, I would recommend the book *Who Made God?* co-edited by Dr. Norman Geisler and myself.

1. Are all of my problems due to my own spiritual maturity (or lack of it)?

Some problems certainly can be caused by a lack of spiritual maturity. Jesus once healed a man who had suffered as an invalid for thirty-eight years. Later Jesus told the man, "Stop sinning or something worse may happen to you" (John 5:14). On the other hand, at another time Jesus healed a man who had been born blind. When others asked Jesus whether the blindness had been caused by the man's own sin or that of his parents, Jesus replied, "Neither this man nor his parents sinned, but this happened so that the work of God might be displayed in his life" (John 9:3).

Many troubles come to us in order to test our faith—to reveal whether it is genuine (1 Peter 1:6–7). God wants to use other problems to help us mature in our walk with Christ (Hebrews 12:11). Some difficulties arise because we make poor or unwise choices (1 Corinthians 11:30–32). And hardships often blow into our lives simply because we live in a fallen world (Luke 13:1–5).

But here's the key: God wants to use *all* of these problems, wherever they come from and whatever their nature, to conform us to the image of his Son, Jesus Christ. He wants to take the tragedies and the ecstasies of your life, as well as the disappointments and the great pleasures, and weave them all into a breathtaking tapestry that showcases his glory, love, power, and wisdom.

2. Is faith strong only when it comes easily? Have some men and women of faith struggled to come to that faith? If so, name a few.

Many biblical heroes of the faith reached their high level of spiritual maturity only through great struggle. One thinks of Moses, Gideon, Thomas, and even the apostle Paul. We may often think of the apostles as men of stout faith, but we should remember how often Jesus said to them things like "Where is your faith?" (Luke 8:25), "Are you so dull?" (Mark 7:18), "Do you still not understand?" (Matthew 16:9), and "Why are you so afraid? Do you still have no faith?" (Mark 4:40).

My own father-in-law died with a strong faith, but it came only with struggle. One of his daughters said of him, "He was a man of faith; yet faith didn't come easily to him."

We all struggle when God seems to hide himself — something God has always done with his children (Isaiah 45:15). John the Baptist struggled with this, as did the apostle Peter. John the Baptist, who introduced Jesus to the world, wondered if Jesus really was who he claimed to be once John found himself in prison (Matthew 11:2–3). And Peter, who saw Jesus transfigured before his very eyes, just a short while later denied that he even knew him (Matthew 26:69–74)

So I find it interesting that this same Peter wrote, "And the God of all grace, who called you to his eternal glory in Christ, *after you have suffered a little while*, will himself restore you and make you strong, firm and steadfast" (1 Peter 5:10, italics added). Peter tells us that spiritual strength — that is, a strong faith — comes *after* suffering and struggle, not before.

So do not fear the struggle; rather, embrace it. Embrace it in the knowledge that the Grand Weaver will take all of your struggles, questions, disappointments, and fears and use them to build your faith and increasingly make you into a man or woman who looks like Jesus Christ.

3. *Why can I so readily recognize divine design in other things but seem incapable of seeing God's design in me?*

I once spoke at Johns Hopkins University on the topic of "What Does It Mean to Be Human?" The speaker before me showed the audience two slides, side by side—a photo of the magnificent rose window of York Minster in York, England, and a cross section of human DNA. Both slides evoked gasps, not only because of their beauty, but because they looked very much alike in many astonishing ways.

Why did so many feel such surprise? They did so, I think, because while they expected to see glorious design in the stained-glass window, they did not expect to see such similar symmetry and beauty in the strand of DNA, which many of them assume came about randomly and without a designer. In a sense, they were too close to the design to see it easily.

Just as some find it difficult to recognize design in their biology, so we may find it difficult to recognize the transtemporal design in our lives, since our existence is limited to a sequence of single temporal points. We're just too close to the design to recognize it in ourselves. It's as though, on a trip to St. Peter's Basilica in Rome, we complain that we see nothing whatsoever before us, even as we press our noses firmly against the ceiling of the Sistine Chapel.

The problem becomes worse for many of us because we have cultivated a habitual neglect of the past. When we do not look with an eye toward seeing, no wonder we notice only accident and chaos. If we want to see the design being created by the Grand Weaver, we have to look for it.

Of course, sometimes we cannot see this design merely by looking. We may not recognize any design at all while the tapestry is being woven. In fact, we may recognize the design only in retrospect, only as it nears completion. Still, we will not see it at all if we do not train ourselves to look.

4. How can I see God's pattern in my life unfold, even when I am in pain?

I see three distinct steps to take in order to ascertain God's pattern unfolding in one's life:

Step 1: Allow God to make your heart tender. Responding appropriately to hurts and disappointments makes one sensitive to God's personal interaction. God uses your hurts and disappointments to shape your heart and the way you feel about reality. The hurts you live through also shape you; there is no way around it. At the end of your life, your heart will either have become coarse and desensitized, have been crushed under the weight of disappointment, or have been made tender by that which makes the heart of God tender.

Step 2: Make your mind strong through faith. Learn to trust in God's control and depend on his providence. Acting out such a faith helps avoid tension with respect to God's purpose. Faith is a thing of the mind. If you do not believe that God is in control and has formed you for a purpose, then you will flounder on the high seas of purposelessness and drown in its rushing currents. God has made it imperative, in the design of life, to be willing to trust beyond yourself. Walking by faith means to follow Someone else who knows more than you do, Someone who is not only all-powerful but also good.

Step 3: See the world through the lens of Jesus' sacrifice. Fix your tender heart and your faithful mind on the cross of Jesus, and through it, see the world according to God's pattern. You must learn to see the world of pain through the eyes of the One who best understands it, not merely as pain but as brokenness and separation. God shows us through his love, demonstrated at the cross, that he alone bridged the distance between him and us. That's how God enables us to see this world through Calvary. If you don't see it this way, you will never see it God's way and the threads of the masterpiece he is weaving of your life will always pull away from the design.

Once you take these three steps — allow God to make your heart tender, make your mind strong through faith, and consider the cross to be the aortic nerve of life — you can begin to see God's pattern in you. In this way you can become an instrument of consolation to others who hurt.

5. *What does the Bible mean by "perfection," and what does it mean to "have the work of God displayed" in my personal suffering?*

Perfection is not a change in the essential character but rather the completion of a course. For us it is a process and not a state. Although we are fallen and exist in various states of imperfection, nevertheless we may be made perfect by God through the various trials and sufferings that come our way — just as a person, though plagued by a bad left knee and a few broken ribs, can still maneuver an obstacle course to its completion. In this sense, even Jesus — who never sinned — was "made perfect" through suffering (Hebrews 2:10). This must mean that while some perfections are eternally unchangeable, other perfections are time laden, not only for the one demonstrating it but, more important, for the completion of the one witnessing it. The Bible calls Job, for example, a "blameless" (some translations, "perfect") man, even though he was far from sinless. God allowed tests not only to shape Job but also to give to us who follow him an example of how an upright person works his way through pain and hurt.

6. *What central feature of the gospel addresses suffering?*

The hill of Calvary is the center point of the gospel. All the suffering of the world converged there in that single act of sacrifice when Jesus Christ, the One without sin, took the penalty of our sin and accepted the ultimate in suffering—separation from his Father—so that we might be brought to him. That was the lowest point of the incarnate Christ—to be separated from the Father while still in the center of the Father's will. We can therefore understand and deal with suffering only when we see it through the eyes of the One who defines good and evil, comfort and suffering, and who went to the cross to deal with it.

7. *Should I make it my life's goal to be number one in all that I do?*

A constant striving to be number one is often the very thing that ultimately destroys a person. Such a pursuit can never deliver the fulfillment you seek. A professional athlete or ballplayer has a genius all his or her own, and it is to be admired. But we make a huge mistake in taking our cue from competitive sports and applying the guidelines that govern success in sports to the way in which we measure success in other areas of life. When we define "success" in such narrow terms, we allow pride and the corrupt desires it fosters to lead us down blind alleys and off steep cliffs. Success is about much more than attracting envious peers and an adoring public. True success comes in finding and living out God's design for your life—and God, in his extraordinary way, can bring "failure" to you or even cast you into prison to help you find your divine calling.

8. *What is a calling, and what is the starting point for determining my calling?*

A calling is simply God's shaping of your burden and his beckoning you to your service to him in the place and pursuit of his choosing. Finding your home in your service to Christ is key to noticing the threads that God has designed just for you. When you find it, you inevitably feel that hand-in-glove sensation. Finding it gives you the security of knowing that you are utilizing your gifts and your will to *God's* ends first, not yours. When you align your will with God's will, his calling on you has found its home. A true call of God puts a tug on your soul that you cannot escape, no matter how unattractive the cost of following it may feel. And what is the starting point for this process? The Bible leaves us in no doubt: do what you know to be God's will, and then watch how he will lead you into what you do not yet know. You are God's temple; so act like it. God reinforces his call as you respond to his nod.

9. *How does determining my call help me pull together different aspects of my life?*

I believe that three primary areas of life get pulled together in determining your call. First, determining your call meets your *spiritual* need. You cannot discover your call without first knowing that your sins have been forgiven through faith in the finished work of Christ on your behalf. Second, it addresses your *physical* needs. God will never call you to do anything for which he will not fully equip you. And third, it engages your *intellectual* needs and gives you the tools to instruct you on your journey. These three are not mutually exclusive. God is an immensely practical Being who promises to guide you by using many means, including reason and wisdom.

10. What is the fundamental difference in framework between a naturalistic worldview and an atheistic worldview?

"Atheism" negates theism and so denies the existence of God. "Naturalism" tries to describe everything in human experience exclusively through empirical inquiry in the sciences. So while the first clearly rejects God, the second finds the idea of God irrelevant, since God cannot be subjected to standard scientific inquiry. The fundamental difference between both the naturalistic and atheistic worldviews and the religious worldview is the moral framework. While a naturalist or an atheist may choose to be a moral person, their worldviews provide no compelling rational reason why one should not be amoral. Reason simply does not dictate here. Pragmatism and personal preference may, but reason alone doesn't allow one to defend one way over another.

11. Is the Christian faith about more than just morality?

The Christian faith, simply stated, reminds us that our fundamental problem is not moral; it is spiritual. A moral life alone cannot bridge what separates us from God. This is the cardinal difference between the moralizing religions and Jesus' offer to us. Jesus does not offer to make bad people good but to make dead people alive. In every religion except Christianity, morality is a means of attainment. In Christianity, God must act first to make us spiritually alive; only then can we progress in our moral efforts. When God gave the Ten Commandments to the Hebrew people, his extraordinary first line gave the basis for those laws: "I am the LORD your God, who brought you out of Egypt, out of the land of slavery. You shall have no other gods before me" (Exodus 20:2–3). To miss that preamble is to miss the entire content of the Mosaic law. It is here that the Hebrew-Christian worldview stands distinct and definitively different from all other religious traditions: redemption precedes morality, and not the other way around.

12. What, then, is the place of morality in my Christian walk if it is not the cause of my salvation?

The moral law in every legal code other than in the Judeo-Christian tradition separates people (the Laws of Manu, the caste system, the Code of Hammurabi with the slave/owner distinction). In Islam, the violator is inferior to the obedient one. By contrast, in the Hebrew-Christian tradition, the law unifies. None of us are made righteous before God by keeping the law. The moral law can be truly understood for what it is—a mirror that indicts and calls the heart to seek God's help—only after redemption. This is what makes moral reasoning the fruit of spiritual understanding and not the cause of it. So what place does the moral law have? Your moral framework is critical in the respect you show for yourself and your fellow human beings. Morality is the fruit of your knowledge of God, conscious or otherwise. Morality is still the ground from within which the creative spirit of art and other disciplines may grow. The moral law also serves as a profound reminder that there is no contradiction in God; it stands as a consistent, contradiction-free expression of God's character. If you violate this law, you bring contradiction into your life and your life begins to fall apart. Pure morality points you to the purest One of all; and the purer your habits, the closer to God you will come. So let all goodness draw you nearer and let all goodness flow from you to point others to the Source of all goodness.

13. *What kinds of flawed "spirituality" seem most popular today?*

I see three principal forms of flawed spirituality reigning today: traditionalism, legalism, and superstition.

Traditionalism. Many sects and groups build their traditions around revered human sayings and laws. Some of them can be serious, and some are almost comical, but all are accepted and held with the same tenacity. Over the centuries, spiritual ceremony tends to become more important than the thing it was designed to facilitate. Jesus consistently raised questions about sacrifice and ceremony, as did the Old Testament prophets. The apostle Paul even says that the enemy of our souls delights to use ceremony and ritual based on falsehood to control and enslave us to error (see 1 Corinthians 10:14–22).

Legalism. We human beings are incurably religious. We long to worship and will even create our own objects of worship. Legalists suggest that if you keep the law meticulously, somehow you will be protected from God's wrath. Jesus clashed repeatedly with those who "lived by the law" and who used the law to condemn others but who never saw the spirit behind the law. Legalism tends to create a culture of fear even as it spawns attitudes of smug superiority.

Superstition. This type of spirituality controls millions of people worldwide. Those under its sway believe that they must do, say, or practice certain oaths or activities in a very particular way; otherwise something bad will certainly happen to them. These superstitions may be of very recent or very ancient origin, and they may be unique to the individual rather than passed down through the generations. The superstitious do not worry about violating laws as much as they fear bringing misfortune on themselves by failing to behave in a way that the gods or spirits or fate or some other force demands. Bad omens and bad luck control their lives.

All three flawed expressions of spirituality have similar results: they enslave people to an unproductive and unsatisfying way of living; they cause them to live in fear a great deal of the time; and they focus attention on their own ability to provide for their safety and well-being rather than nurturing trust in the living God, in whom alone human beings can find life.

14. In trying to find God's design for my life, is any one "thread" most important? If so, where can I find this thread?

By far, the most important thread is *truth*. In no segment of society can we survive without truth. Whether it's in the courts or in our marriages, we simply cannot live without the truth. Truth will sooner or later catch up to us, and we will have to pay its dues. When truth dies, people get sacrificed at the altar of pragmatism and manipulated by words in the ugly human game of one-upmanship. Without truth, the threads do not make a beautiful design. Without truth, spirituality is nothing more than a hopeless confession that sheer matter alone does not answer life's deepest hungers. Truth is the thread that separates true spirituality from false spirituality. Spirituality does not give relevance to life; rather, truth gives relevance to spirituality. And where do you find the thread of truth? Jesus provided the answers when he said, "If you hold to my teaching, you are really my disciples. Then you will know the truth, and the truth will set you free" (John 8:31–32). Jesus also said, "I am the way and the truth and the life" (John 14:6). With Jesus the Truth in your life, this most important thread holds all the others together. The Word, the Truth, Christ's person, and true freedom are inextricably connected. Break that design, and you break life. Honor that design, and you find true freedom.

15. I've noticed that humanity often seems to swing between extremes. Can you name some philosophies that have gone to an extreme?

The terminology is big   rationalism, empiricism, existentialism, postmodernism. In each of these ways of looking at reality, one thread dominated and obliterated the others. In rationalism it was *reason* above all else. In empiricism it was *scientific single-vision*. In existentialism it was the *triumph of the will* in the face of despair. In postmodernism it was the *absence of absolute truth* as something possible to know. Each has its significant weakness. The scientist, for example, must test his or her theories through observation and verification— but how does one find out whether a man or a woman ought to honor his or her marital vows? That requires a worldview, one that must be subjected to the tests of truth. Unfortunately, none of these extremes provide such a comprehensive worldview. Remarkably, however, God gives some of these emphases their rightful place.

16. When God saves a person, what changes should we expect to see?

When God brings someone to salvation, the most remarkable thing we see is that God transforms the person's hungers—sometimes gradually and sometimes immediately, but always certainly. God doesn't merely change what the individual does, but what he or she *wants* to do. This is the work of the Holy Spirit within every believer—"to will and to act according to [God's] good purpose" (Philippians 2:13). A big part of this good purpose is to make us into new people. So God gives believers a new heart and a new spirit (Ezekiel 18:31), a new birth (1 Peter 1:3), a new life (Acts 5:20), a new mind (Ephesians 4:23), a new name (Revelation 2:17), and a new nature (Ephesians 4:24), all of which together result in a new creation (2 Corinthians 5:17). The apostle Paul sums it up nicely when he writes that Jesus "gave himself for us to redeem us from all wickedness and to purify for himself a people that are his very own, *eager to do what is good*" (Titus 2:14, emphasis added). A believer makes new choices that help shape God's design into something beautiful.

17. How can I determine whether something that I find attractive is a legitimate or illegitimate pursuit?

Getting sidetracked into secondary pursuits is the bane of our lives. Joshua reminds us that we must each deliberately choose whom we will serve (Joshua 24:15). That's why it's crucial to identify, describe, and mark down your life's goal. It becomes the measuring stick to determine whether attractions and distractions are legitimate or illegitimate. Susanna Wesley, the mother of John and Charles Wesley, once gave wise counsel here: "Whatever weakens your reasoning, impairs the tenderness of your conscience, obscures your sense of God, or takes away your relish for spiritual things; in short, if anything increases the authority and power of the flesh over the Spirit, then that to you becomes sin, however good it is in itself."

18. How can I begin to discipline my will?

The answer is easy, although the practice is anything but. You must begin with self-crucifixion. In effect, you go to your own funeral and bury your self-will so that God's will reigns supremely in your heart. There is no way for the will to be empowered to do God's will until it first dies to its own desires and the Holy Spirit brings a fresh power within. The gospel message insists that the Holy Spirit does the work of the new birth within us. Because of the Spirit's power within, the follower of Jesus Christ gains the capacity to do God's will. It is only in and through the power of the Holy Spirit that the Christian walk is even possible. I remain utterly convinced that when you work under God's will and your will submits to that will, you become a different person before people. And so I like to speak of the ABCDs of a willful walk with the Lord:

A. *Ask without pettiness.* God promises the Holy Spirit to those who simply and sincerely ask him for that gift of God. If the will to serve God is there, the Holy Spirit must both prompt the prayer and empower the will.

B. *Being before doing.* A Christian is really "a Christ one." I am a child of God who must be that child in my own understanding. I am not my own; I belong to God. Resting in that knowledge, I know what it is to be God's. I then pursue doing God's will, and by his grace he enables my will.

C. Convictions without compromise. The will is both the framer of your convictions and the efficient cause in honoring those convictions. Setting these convictions in place gives you guidelines of where to draw the lines. A conviction is not merely an opinion. It is something rooted so deeply in the conscience that to change a conviction would be to change who you are.

D. Disciplines without drudgery. Discipline always seems like a weight around our necks. But if you can come to see the need and the fruit of discipline, then you can begin to see why it offers such great rewards. The Lord tells us that he disciplines those he loves, which means the undisciplined life is an unloved life. Focus on honoring God with everything you have, and watch the peace it brings.

19. *How can I best define my ultimate identity?*

Our identity is derived from relationship. We carry within us a deep-seated bond to those we love and know and represent. Our identity means something more than just our separate individual lives. For Christians, who we are is always defined by "Whose" we are first. My name is identified with Christ's name. This explains why the apostle Paul so frequently addresses his letters not merely to the believers in this or that town but "to those sanctified in Christ Jesus and called to be holy, together with all those everywhere who call on the name of our Lord Jesus Christ—their Lord and ours" (1 Corinthians 1:2). Your ultimate identity is wrapped up not in your ethnicity or your gender or your socioeconomic background or your vocation or your age or your current living situation or anything so temporal or changeable as that, but in your identification as a son or daughter of God, as a co-heir with Christ and a citizen of heaven. *That* is who you are, if through faith in the risen Jesus you are "in Christ"—and that can never change.

20. *What do you consider to be the most important aspects of worship?*

I see three principal realities in worship: mystery, community, and liturgy.

Mystery. The mystery inherent in Christian worship is the adoration of the Holy Trinity in the reverential taking of the elements in the Lord's Supper. Thomas Merton described this mystery so well. Of his first Communion he wrote,

> In the temple of God that I had just become, the once eternal and pure sacrifice was offered up to the God dwelling in me. The sacrifice of God to God. Now, Christ born in me, a new Bethlehem, and sacrificed in me his new Calvary, and risen in me: offering me to the Father, in himself, asking the Father, my Father and his, to receive me into his infinite and special love—not the love he has for all things that exist, for mere existence is a token of God's love, but the love of those creatures who are drawn to him in and with the power of his own love for himself.

This is the mystery, the majesty, and the grandeur of holy Communion—God's love shed in our hearts to keep us from fragmentation and dissolution.

Community. The church is supposed to be a healing community. Sadly, the community of the early church— the one that shared everything and held all things in common—didn't last long. Over time, jealousies and insensitivities won the day, and they went from "see how they love each other" to division and comparing gifts and expressing their feelings of superiority over each other. True "comm-union" and "comm-unity" does not ignore diversity. Diversity is recognized and valued, as in the Godhead, but the diversities are brought together because of what is held in common—the worship of the triune God and the shared meanings of the family of God. The members of a community come together in communion to worship, their individual lives attuned, first and foremost, to God. Then their joint expression can take on certain beneficial forms.

Liturgy. The liturgy of the church has five components: the Lord's Supper, teaching, prayer, praise, and giving. For more, see question 23 below.

21. *Thomas Merton once said, "We cannot be at peace with others because we are not at peace with ourselves, and we cannot be at peace with ourselves because we are not at peace with God." What does this mean?*

In short, the break of communion with God was the cause of our break with one another, even within individual families. Humanity will never find unity until it can understand the reason for its brokenness and the expression of Jesus' broken body and shed blood in the Lord's Supper. Jesus was broken so that we might be mended. "Eat the bread, drink from the cup" expresses renewed fellowship with God from which we begin to experience renewed fellowship with our fellow human beings. The chief question here, however, is not just what all this means, but whether each of us, individually, has experienced it for ourselves. Have you?

22. *What do you think is the most effective way to help someone overcome some stubborn sin or persistent failure?*

I can't help but think of my younger years in ministry when I carelessly uttered words of castigation against certain persons, things, and behavior, no doubt plunging verbal blades into already sore spots. We tend to focus on each other's mistakes and sins, and so we hurt and injure the already injured. We knock out the already knocked down. We lose the shared meanings of pain, and so the shared meanings of victory become occasions for jealousy. It is appallingly easy for most of us to lash out and cut and condemn with prophetic zeal. Pulling someone down is easy; building someone up is difficult. It takes a mature and patient heart to heal with a tender touch, yet without compromising convictions. But wasn't that exactly the way our Lord handled the Samaritan woman and the woman with the alabaster jar of perfume (see John 4:7–26; Matthew 26:6–13)? Without justifying their mistakes, Jesus brought hope and healing, not condemnation and reprimand. Since Jesus calls us his friends, disciples, brothers, and co-heirs, shouldn't we therefore strive through the power of the Spirit to do likewise? "But that is not my natural bent!" you may protest. I daresay it wasn't the natural bent of the apostle Paul either. You cannot read about his early life in the book of Acts without imagining him as a fiery, conviction-driven, no-nonsense defender of what he believed to be the truth. And yet, as the Spirit worked in his life, he could write the following to some young Christian friends: "we were gentle among you, like a mother caring for her little children. We loved you so much that we were delighted to share with you not only the gospel of God but our lives as well, because you had become so dear to us" (1 Thessalonians 2:7–8). If our goal is to partner with God in order to change lives, this is the way to do it.

23. *What does it mean to worship in spirit and in truth?*

The book of Acts gives us the five components of worship: the Lord's Supper, teaching, prayer, praise, and giving.

The Lord's Supper. Taking part in the Lord's Supper is a communal act expressing within a community the fellowship to which God calls us all. The church will never culminate worship until the Communion cup has been drunk to the last dregs. And finally the day will come when we will drink of that cup together in heaven. The oneness of the Trinity and the oneness of our communion with the triune God is the only hope for our fractured lives to be mended and for our fractured societies and fractured races to come together.

Teaching. Without biblical teaching, the rest of the components of worship become prone to heretical expressions. Teaching guides and guards the integrity of worship, gives understanding of how to be a worshiping community, and calls us to remember how God has led in the past. Teaching makes it possible to prepare the children of the community to understand their faith and to pass it on to the next generation.

Prayer. More than anything else, prayer enables you to see your own heart and brings you into alignment with God's heart. Prayer is not a monologue; nor is it only imagining that you are communing with God. Rather, it is a dialogue in which God makes you his dream. It is truly the treasured gift of Christians, designed to help followers of Jesus love God for who he is, not for what they may get out of him.

Praise. The last book of the New Testament pictures the church at worship and praise in the new heaven and the new earth (Revelation 7:9–17). It is a glorious scene, where every tribe and nation and people speak with one voice and one language—the language of the soul—to the glory of God. Each redeemed soul focuses not on itself but on the God who created it. That is when culture finds its most sublime and supreme expression of shared meaning.

Giving. A heart that truly worships is a heart that gives its best to God in time and substance. A heart that truly worships gives generously to the causes of God. To consume the best for yourself and give the crumbs to God is blasphemy. I have to wonder whether we may wake up someday to find out that all our incestuous spending on ourselves and our building of excessively luxurious places of worship—while we ignore, for the most part, the hurting and the deprived of the world—has terribly wounded God's tender heart. I also wonder if the world does not take us seriously in our mission because we spend more and more on ourselves and give less and less to the world in need. If we are to be true worshipers, we must learn the art and the heart of giving.

24. Does God have some kind of preeminent goal for my life? If so, what is it and how can I reach it?

The Scriptures very clearly declare that God has chosen us to be conformed to the image of his Son, Jesus Christ (Romans 8:29; 2 Corinthians 3:18). While we will never be like Jesus in essence, God calls us to be like him in our reflective splendor. God has given us the privilege to be Christ's image bearers and to reflect his splendor— his perfection, his holiness, his transcendent majesty. And since our ultimate destiny is to become like Jesus,

our ultimate home is heaven. We will be where Jesus is.
That simple description of being at home with God is
the ultimate destiny of the follower of Jesus Christ. God
calls us his children and his friends, and finally, he calls
us home to be with him. All those who name the name of
Christ will be at home with God. That's our destiny.

25. *Why do we so crave a loving touch? What hazards and*
pleasures does such a longing create for us?

Of all the sensitivities we have, the sense of touch is the
one we long for the most. We crave the tender touch of a
loved one, a soft caress to let us know that we are valued,
esteemed, cherished. To feel is to be alive; to not feel is
to be dead in the truest sense of the term. In fact, one of
the most important faculties we have is the ability to feel,
whether in the physical or in the emotional realm. When
our bodies hurt, we feel pain — that is the hazard. When
we hold a loved one's hand or kiss a beloved face, we feel
love — that is the glory. And even as we live with such
discord, our souls are given hints of the harmony that we
long for and await. I believe that our longings provide us
with a hint of our eternal home in heaven and of God's
consummate touch — the one we will feel when God
wipes away every tear from our eyes (Revelation 21:4).
The glory of the sensitivity of touch (both in the physical
and the emotional/spiritual sense) looks to be, in its most
potent and revealed, a powerful feeling of longing for what
lies beyond the mortal threshold.

Walking from East to West

God in the Shadows

Ravi Zacharias with R. S. B. Sawyer

Ravi Zacharias has lived an extraordinary life. He has walked with great leaders, slept in the villages and homes of the poor, and crossed continents to bring the good news of the gospel to the world.

Already a man of two worlds by the time he was twenty, Ravi never dreamed that God would lead him from his birth home in India to Canada and the United States, and eventually to a platform on the world stage. In *Walking from East to West*, he tells his life story, a deeply personal journey into his past. Dr. Zacharias invites you back to the southern India of his early childhood, and into his troubled youth in the sophisticated capital city of Delhi. He recalls the importance of a mother's love and his difficult relationship with his father. He tells about his long search for truth in wrestling with Eastern thought and the newer ideas of Christianity, the cry for help in a dark moment when he tried to take his own life — and the dramatic turning point that led to a life lived for Christ.

This is a story about a remarkable man. Yet it is also everyone's story of belief — how it begins, how it grows, and the daily struggles associated with it. *Walking from East to West* is the heartfelt story of one man's discovery that God is the author of our destinies, no matter how dark the shadows that hide the light.

Hardcover, Jacketed 0-310-25915-0

Pick up a copy today at your favorite bookstore!

 ZONDERVAN®
.com

Who Made God?

And Answers to Over 100 Other Tough Questions of Faith

Ravi Zacharias and Norman Geisler, General Editors

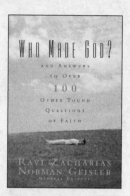

In the quest for the truth, you need to know what you believe and why you believe it. *Who Made God?* offers accessible answers to over 100 commonly asked apologetic questions. Bringing together the best in evangelical apologists, this guide is standard equipment for Christians who want to understand and talk about their faith intelligently.

Part 1 answers tough questions about the Christian faith such as:

• Who made God? • How can there be three persons in one God? • What is God's ultimate purpose in allowing evil? • Where did the universe come from? • How long are the days of creation in Genesis? • Did Jesus rise from the dead? • Are the records of Jesus' life reliable? • Does the Bible have errors in it?

Part 2 answers tough questions about other faiths, including Islam, Mormonism, Hinduism, Transcendental Meditation, Yoga, Reincarnation, Buddhism, and Black Islam. Relevant stories, questions for reflection and discussion, and a comprehensive list of suggested resources help you dig deeper so you can be prepared to give careful answers that explain the reasons for your faith.

Softcover 0-310-24710-1

Pick up a copy today at your favorite bookstore!

Is Your Church Ready?

Motivating Leaders to Live an Apologetic Life

Ravi Zacharias and Norman Geisler, General Editors

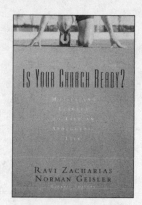

A ministry resource for motivating all Christians to become thoughtful apologists of their faith.

Although apologetics is as crucial today as it has ever been, the classical model for defending the faith often seems irrelevant to the twenty-first century where people listen with their eyes and think with their emotions. *Is Your Church Ready?* presents a team of highly qualified Christian thinkers—including Ravi Zacharias, John Guest, Peter Grant, J. Budziszewski, Judy Salisbury, and Dean Halverson—who build a case for the place of apologetics in the local church, home, and school. Using personal examples and illustrations they address:

- How to answer objections to Christianity
- How to equip children in the home and prepare youth to remain committed to
- Christ after they leave for college
- How to reach international students and the foreign-born

Included are discussion questions and a "Church Leaders Annotated Resource Guide" to the best books, articles, organizations, and websites on the subject.

Hardcover, Jacketed 0-310-25061-7

Pick up a copy today at your favorite bookstore!

ZONDERVAN®
.com

We want to hear from you. Please send your comments about this book to us in care of zreview@zondervan.com. Thank you.

ZONDERVAN.com/
AUTHORTRACKER
follow your favorite authors